THE KINGFISHER BOOK OF
RELIGIONS

In this book, CE stands for
Common Era and BCE for
Before Common Era, with the
Common Era beginning in the year 0

The publishers would like to thank the following editorial
consultants for their help:
Dr M.A.Zaki Badawi, Principal, The Muslim College, London
Dr Sue Hamilton, Department of Theology and
Religious Studies, King's College, London
The Reverend Leslie Houlden, formerly Professor of New
Testament Studies, King's College, London
Dr Nicholas de Lange, Fellow, Wolfson College, Cambridge
Dr Stewart McFarlane, visiting professor at Chung Hwa
Institute of Buddhist Studies, Taiwan
Dr Eleanor Nesbitt, Lecturer in Religions and
Education, University of Warwick
Ranchor Prime, member of the International Consultancy
on Religion, Education and Culture
Rabbi Sylvia Rothschild, Bromley and
District Reform Synagogue
Inderjit Singh, editor of the *Sikh Messenger*

Edited and designed by Toucan Books Limited, London

For Kingfisher
Managing editor Miranda Smith
Art director Mike Davis
DTP co-ordinator Nicky Studdart

KINGFISHER

Kingfisher Publications Plc
New Penderel House, 283-288 High Holborn, London WC1V 7HZ

First published by Kingfisher Publications Plc 1999

2 4 6 8 10 9 7 5 3 1

ITR/0599/MDS/MA/JWA157

Copyright © Kingfisher Publications Plc 1999

A CIP catalogue record for this book is available from the British Library

ISBN 0-7534-0342-0

Colour separations by Modern Age
Printed in Hong Kong

THE KINGFISHER BOOK OF
RELIGIONS

Festivals, ceremonies and beliefs from around the world

TREVOR BARNES

KINGƒISHER

CONTENTS

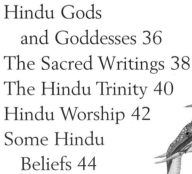

WHAT IS RELIGION?

Some questions are easy to answer. "What time is it?" "What colour is grass?" "What is two plus two?" Other questions are much harder. "Where was I before I was born?" "Where will I go when I die?" "Who created the world?" Such questions (and more) have been asked throughout the history of humanity, and at different stages in their development, different tribes, societies and peoples have supplied different answers that made sense at the time.

> **"You shall love your neighbour as yourself."**
>
> Leviticus 19:18

Religion tries to answer the big questions in life. "Why is there suffering in the world?" "Is there life after death?" "How should I live my life on Earth?" "If God created the world who created God?" Of course you do not have to be religious to ask – philosophy and science pose the same questions. But for most of our history, philosophy and science have themselves been part of the religious understanding of the world. Both have shared the deeply human sense of mystery at the wonder of creation.

Above This Nepali girl is believed to be a living goddess, a reincarnation of Kumari, goddess of power. At the age of 12 or 13 (at puberty) she resumes a normal life and another girl is chosen by the Hindu priests.

There are things that cannot be fully explained by our intellect or our reason. The Christian writer C S Lewis once gave this example. Imagine you are in a room with a dead body at night. The chances are you would feel nervous or even afraid. But why? A dead body cannot hurt you, make fun of you, or say cruel things to you.

Right These Muslim girls are learning the Koran in Arabic at an evening class in a mosque in the north of England.

Above Santiago de Compostela in northern Spain is traditionally thought to house the bones of St James. Since the Middle Ages it has been an important place of pilgrimage for Christians from all over the world.

Right A Jewish family recalls the events of the Exodus – the deliverance of the Jews from slavery in Egypt – at the annual Passover meal.

In fact, the dead body cannot do you any harm, and yet it has a strange power to generate troubling thoughts. "If the body is dead, where has its life gone?" "When I am dead, will I end up there, too?" "Will the body come back to haunt me as a ghost?" The strange, irrational sensation of awe and unease that a 'harmless' motionless corpse provokes has been called 'numinous'. That is to say, it suggests a divine or spiritual presence outside ourselves. We may feel the presence of the numinous at any time – in a mosque, or a temple, or gazing up at the stars in the night sky. We may feel it at the birth of a brother or sister, or at the death of a grandparent. In prehistoric times, people probably felt it when thunder roared or lightning struck. It is that strange 'something' that we cannot satisfactorily explain, but that suggests another world beyond the one we can see. A sense of the numinous is at the heart of all the world's religions.

> **"Not one of you is a believer until he loves for his brother what he loves for himself."**
>
> *Hadith* of the Prophet Muhammad

In the name of religion

Some religions believe in one god who created heaven and Earth. Others believe in the existence of several gods who take strange forms and control human lives. Some, like Buddhism, do not believe in the idea of a god at all. Great cruelty has been committed in the name of religion, but also great acts of kindness and self-sacrifice. At their best, religions teach that proper respect for the divine should be mirrored in proper respect for the whole of creation.

THE STORY OF THE WORLD'S RELIGIONS

What is the link between a golden temple in northwest India and a huge red rock in central Australia? What does a totem pole in the United States have in common with a circle of stones in the south of England? Why do millions of people every year make a special journey to a wall in Jerusalem, a church in Rome and a black cube in Mecca? The answer to all these questions involves one word – religion, a phenomenon common to all people in all times. From Salt Lake City, headquarters of the Church of Jesus Christ of Latter-day Saints (Mormons) in the USA, to Kandy in Sri Lanka where it is believed that the Buddha's tooth is housed in a famous temple, people have constructed buildings and monuments to their faith. Or, as with Mount Tai in China, they have looked to elements of the natural world in awe and wonder. The common link is a sense of the sacred in life.

Above Religions such as Christianity and Islam have large groups of followers in many parts of the world. Others, like the Chinese religions, tend to be confined to one particular region.

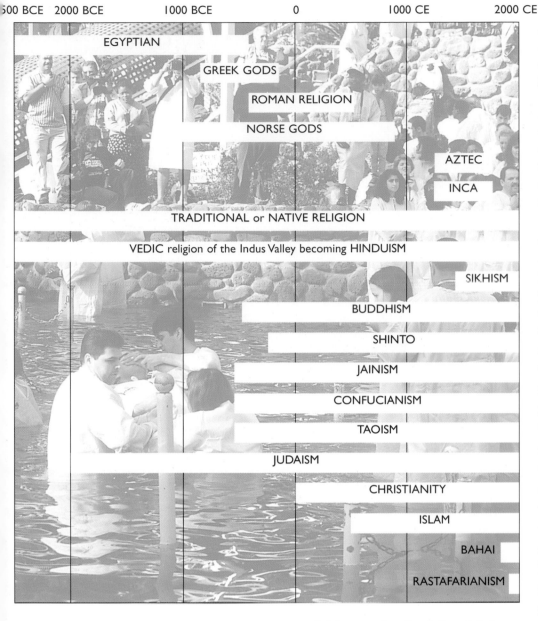

500 BCE 2000 BCE   1000 BCE   0   1000 CE   2000 CE

EGYPTIAN

GREEK GODS

ROMAN RELIGION

NORSE GODS

AZTEC

INCA

TRADITIONAL or NATIVE RELIGION

VEDIC religion of the Indus Valley becoming HINDUISM

SIKHISM

BUDDHISM

SHINTO

JAINISM

CONFUCIANISM

TAOISM

JUDAISM

CHRISTIANITY

ISLAM

BAHAI

RASTAFARIANISM

Left Some religions (Christianity and Islam, for example) are easily dated since the historical facts of their founders' lives are well documented. Others, like the religion of the ancient Egyptians, are more difficult to locate in time. Similarly, the religion the West has come to know as Hinduism has not always existed in that form. It developed over long periods of time, making precise dating impossible.

When did religion begin?

Religion is as old as humankind, which first looked to powers outside itself for protection and reassurance. Early peoples worshipped the Sun and the rain as sources of life and fertility, and trembled as the thunder seemed to be roaring its displeasure. They asked unseen gods for help in times of need and thanked them in times of plenty. The gods they worshipped may have been illusions but the comfort they brought was real. For many millions of people, faith is as real today as it was in the time of Moses, the Buddha, Mahavira, Jesus Christ, the Prophet Muhammad or Guru Nanak.

Religion in people's lives

Religion in one form or another plays a part in the lives of most of the world's population, sometimes dictating what they eat, where they live, what they wear, who they marry and how they think. Fired by the same religious impulse, believers do different things. Buddhist monks shave their heads, for example, while many Sikhs never cut their hair at all. Some worship with loud music and vibrant dance, while others sit still in complete silence. And, while some religions will hold out the promise of a future life in the hereafter, all religions (whether they believe in one God, many gods, or no god) will encourage a life requiring goodness in the here and now.

Left Most religions have their sacred places, some made by humans like Aztec pyramids, others natural like Uluru (Ayers Rock) or Mount Tai in China.

ANCIENT RELIGIONS: AN INTRODUCTION

Remember that what we call ancient religions were modern religions once. In their time they satisfied many of the same spiritual longings and answered many of the same spiritual questions that living religion does today. But ancient religions died out when they failed to meet humanity's deepest needs.

Mythology or religion

The gods of ancient Greece and Rome, the deities of ancient Egypt, and the superhuman figures of the ancient Scandinavian world live on in myths and legends, but they have generally lost the power to connect with us. The God of the Hebrew Bible parts the waves to let His chosen people flee from Egypt. He sustains them with food from heaven. The God of the New Testament so loved the world that He sacrificed His only Son to save it. The God of the Koran is compassionate and gives humanity a special place in His creation. By contrast, the Greek and Roman gods are worshipped and feared but rarely loved. They change shape and appear on Earth but seldom intervene in human affairs, giving the impression that they are distant, cold and sometimes even cruel.

Spirits in nature

The natural world played a large part in shaping early religions. The Sun and the rain were sources of fertility that influenced lives. It was only a short step from there to worshipping these powerful elements as divine beings who controlled peoples' fates.

Left In ancient times the gods were often associated with the elemental forces of nature. Here the Norse goddess Freya holds her hand to her breast, which symbolizes fruitfulness and fertility.

Below These cave paintings were made by hunters around 17,000BCE in Lascaux, southwest France. By representing the animals in picture form they believed they could exercise some control over them.

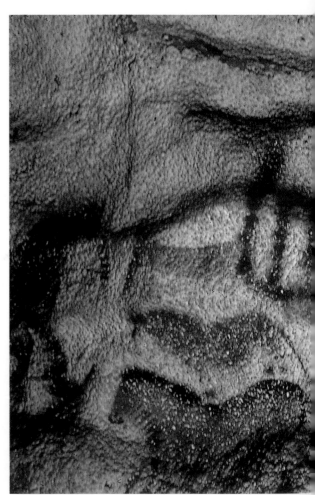

Left Stonehenge, perhaps the most famous of the ancient stone circles, was built between 3000 and 1500BCE on Salisbury Plain in Wiltshire, southwest England. It is believed to have been used for the worship of fertility gods and goddesses, as well as for complex astronomical calculations.

A natural impulse

Cave paintings made around 17,000BCE, such as those in the caves at Lascaux in southwest France, show how early men and women expressed their wonder at the natural world around them. Around this time, female figurines representing a mother goddess began to appear throughout Europe. As stable societies based on farming and agriculture began to emerge, rituals developed to express the relationship between humanity and an unseen spirit world. Eventually, buildings were constructed specifically for prayer and sacrifice, gods and goddesses were given their own temples or shrines, and stories were told to be passed on from generation to generation. And, like the living religions of today, the ancient religions tried to give meaning to the joy, tragedy and mystery of human life.

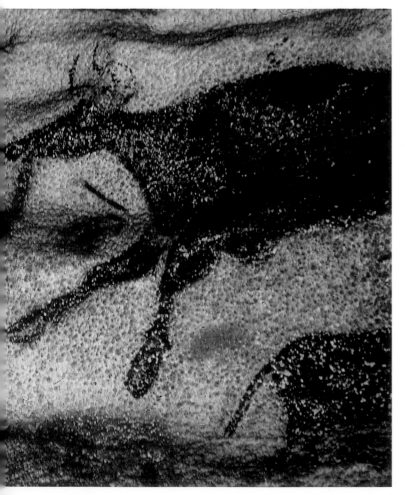

Above Zeus (known to the Romans as Jupiter) was the supreme god of the ancient Greeks. He was believed to be the ultimate ruler of humankind.

ANCIENT EGYPT

The Sun god Ra was a principal deity in ancient Egyptian religion. He was worshipped as the creator of all life and because he lived in the sky he was often depicted with a falcon's head. As a powerful force whose daily journey across the sky controlled everyone's life, he was associated with the ruling pharaohs who became known as the Sons of Ra.

Amun Ra

At various points in the history of ancient Egypt, gods were associated with individual cities. When alliances were made between them the local gods also joined forces. So, when the city of Heliopolis (now El-Matariya), whose protector god was Ra, made a pact with Thebes (now Luxor), whose protector god was Amun, a joint deity emerged known as Amun Ra, who became for a time the ruling god of the whole nation.

Gods and nature

In addition to Amun Ra, there were many other local gods who were associated with natural forces. Isis was the fertility goddess and queen of all the gods. Osiris was her husband, and later combined with Ra to become the supreme god of Egypt and king of the dead. Horus, the sky god, had a hawk's head. Thoth, the Moon god and god of learning, had the head of an ibis, while Anubis, god of the dead, had a jackal's head. Ptah was a creator god and god of craftspeople.

One god

Several attempts were made to control the number of gods, though these were largely resisted by the priests, whose importance depended on them.

Above Isis and her husband Osiris were important deities in the Egyptian pantheon (collection) of gods. It was believed that Osiris was killed by his brother Seth but brought back to life by Isis, queen of the gods. Osiris became king of the dead and ruled the underworld.

Left The solid gold death mask of the young pharaoh Tutankhamun became famous when it was discovered by the British archaeologist Howard Carter in 1922. The contents of Tutankhamun's tomb remained hidden from robbers and were found intact.

Right Many animals, particularly birds and cats, were sacred to the Egyptians, who mummified them and buried them alongside the dead for company in the afterlife. The fertility goddess Bastet was depicted as a cat.

The most successful was by Amenhotep IV (*c.*1379–1362BCE), husband of Queen Nefertiti, who tried to impose a form of monotheism (belief in a single god) based on Aten (the fiery disc of the Sun). Suppressing all other gods and declaring Aten to be the only source of life, he changed his own name to Akhenaten (spirit of Aten) and closed all the temples that were dedicated to other gods.

The afterlife

Akhenaten was succeeded by Tutankhamun, who was only a boy when he ascended the throne. He abandoned the worship of Aten and reinstated the worship of Amun and the other gods. These gods often included the pharaohs themselves, who were given divine status by the priests and were believed to live on after death. The pyramids are symbols of the immortality that they hoped to achieve. When the pharaohs died, their bodies were preserved, or mummified, and buried with their possessions which, it was thought, would be useful to them in the afterlife.

Left The Temple at Luxor (ancient Thebes) was one of the principal sites of worship. It was led by a professional class of priests and headed by the pharaoh himself, who was also thought to be divine.

13

ANCIENT GREECE

The Greeks had many gods, but the focus of their worship was a group of 12 principal deities believed to live on Mount Olympus under the authority of Zeus, the chief among them. Stories of the gods were recited aloud and passed on by word of mouth. Eventually, they were written down in two major works of poetry called the *Iliad* and the *Odyssey*, both attributed to the poet Homer who lived in the 8th century BCE. These epic poems tell of the lives of two heroic men – Achilles and Odysseus – whose adventures show how personal struggle, fate and the influence of the gods work together in human lives. Each god or goddess was believed to have human qualities (such as courage, kindness, fertility, or musical or artistic skill), but behaved in a superhuman way. The gods rewarded good and brave actions, but became angry if people became proud or boastful.

Places of worship
Temples were constructed on the highest part of the city, known as the 'acropolis'. The most famous temple is the Parthenon in Athens, dedicated to the city's patron goddess, Athena the goddess of wisdom.

Above *Zeus was the head of the family of gods on Mount Olympus who were believed to control the weather and to affect the course of people's lives. Hera, his wife, was the goddess of marriage.*

Ares, god of war, the son of Zeus and Hera

Hephaestus, god of fire and metalworking

Aphrodite, goddess of love and beauty

Artemis, goddess of wild beasts and hunting

Right Delphi, on the slopes of Mount Parnassus, was home to the Temple of Apollo, patron of music and poetry, and the god who most symbolized the spirit of ancient Greece.

Below Apollo and (below right) Demeter, goddess of agriculture and harvests. Demeter is associated with cereal crops and traditionally carries a sheaf of wheat.

Ordinary people had shrines to their favourite gods at home, or they worshipped in secret, following what were known as 'mystery religions'. The most famous of these was the cult of Dionysus, the god of wine. People who had been initiated into the mysteries met for a more intense experience of worship and celebration.

New ideas

Gradually, however, poets and philosophers began to think that a literal belief in these distant and indifferent gods was a rather unsatisfactory way of explaining what life was all about. In particular, Socrates, his disciple Plato and Aristotle developed systems of thought that came to be accepted by much of the western world as a truer understanding of how the world works. The gods eventually became part of a mythological world that, although it explained an aspect of human experience, was no longer thought to be historically true.

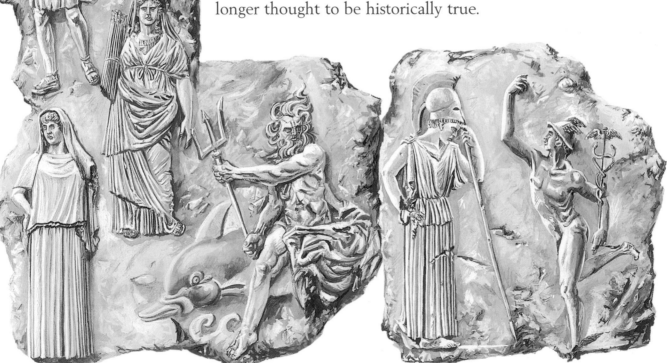

Hestia, goddess of the hearth and family life

Poseidon, god of the sea, with his distinctive trident

Athena, warrior goddess and patron of handicrafts

Hermes, messenger of the gods and the god of travellers

ANCIENT ROME

The word 'religion' comes from the Latin word *religio* which, for the ancient Romans, can be translated as both a bond (between humans and gods) and an obligation (on humans to worship them).

A public religion
Religion was principally a public matter because it was believed that the gods protected the state. The Romans took the Greek gods and adapted them for their own use. So Zeus, the king of the gods, became Jupiter to the Romans, and Hera, his wife, became Juno. The name of Hermes, the messenger of the gods, was changed to Mercury. Athena, goddess of war and wisdom, became Minerva, while Aphrodite, goddess of love and beauty, became Venus. Ares, the god of war, became Mars. Demeter, goddess of the fruitful Earth, became Ceres, while Artemis, goddess of the Moon and hunting, became Diana. Apollo, the god of music, poetry and the arts, kept the same name.

Temple worship
Roman religion was essentially concerned with the performance of specific actions or rites. It did not try to make citizens into better people. Public religious rituals were carried out by a special class of priest, the *pontifex* or *pontifex maximus* (high priest). The ordinary citizens took no part in the rituals; neither were they expected to attend the temple for worship.

Above *Winged Mercury was the messenger of the gods as well as the god of trade and merchants.*

Above This Roman mosaic pavement shows Neptune, the god of the seas and rivers. He rode the waves in a chariot drawn by seahorses and carried a three-pronged spear, or trident, in his hand. When Neptune was in a bad mood he caused earthquakes, storms, disastrous floods, plague and famine.

Below This relief from the Temple of Neptune in Rome shows a sacrifice to Mars, the god of war.

Private devotion

At important times in their lives people consulted an oracle for guidance from a particular god. Often the oracle was situated near water. A favourite was the shrine to Aesculapius, god of healing and the patron of doctors, who carried a staff coiled with snakes. People visited the shrine in the hope that they might be cured of sickness. Other shrines were associated with fertility and were visited by women who wanted to have a child. Divination, or foretelling the future, was also popular. Augurs or people skilled in the art read signs in the stars or in the natural world and claimed to be interpreting the gods' wishes. As in ancient Greece, there were a number of so-called mystery cults that attracted people who wanted a more intense religious experience. For a time Christianity, which overlapped with the many pagan gods and goddesses of the age, was itself considered a mystery religion with its own rites and its own select membership.

Below In Roman houses there were often shrines to the lares and penates, household gods who were associated with farming and food. Here a lar holds a drinking horn and a bowl for offerings made to the gods.

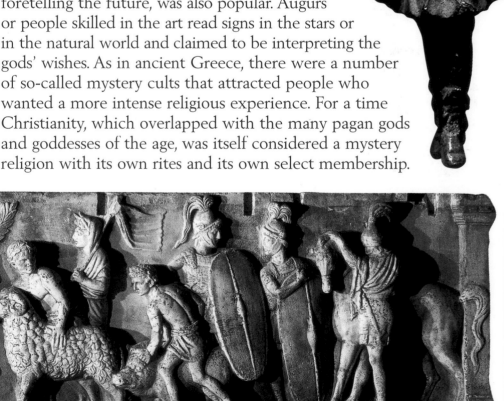

NORSE AND CELTIC RELIGIONS

Norse and Celtic religions developed in the cold countries of north and west Europe and what is now Scandinavia. The climate undoubtedly played a part in forming the character of these gods who, unlike the light and airy gods of the Mediterranean, were often dark and gloomy.

Elemental gods

In Norse religions there were gods of thunder, rain and wind, who were often involved in bloody battles against giants and monsters. Although there is evidence that these gods were worshipped in prehistoric times, they particularly appealed to the Vikings, the traders and warriors who ravaged much of northern Europe between the 8th and 11th centuries CE. Exciting tales of their mythical adventures were recited aloud at banquets and were eventually written down in poems, such as the *Havamal*, or sagas, long tales of heroes and gods.

Norse mythology

The father of the gods, who was the god of war, was Odin (also known as Woden or Wotan). He is often shown riding across the sky on an eight-legged horse. He is said to have had only one eye and to have been fierce in battle and wise in peace. He was served by the Valkyries – warrior maidens who took those who had died in battle up into the heavenly hall reserved for heroes and known as Valhalla. The other great god was Thor. He was the strongest of the principal deities and is depicted as a giant carrying a mighty hammer.

Above *The Druids were ancient Celtic priests and magicians. They worshipped in sacred clearings in the forest, or by lakes and springs, and cut mistletoe as a sign of fertility. They were thought to practise human sacrifice.*

Left *The traditional Celtic cross was a religious symbol before Christianity arrived in Europe. The Christianity of the early 5th- and 6th-century missionaries, such as Patrick and Columba, was influenced by Celtic culture, in particular by its concern for the natural world.*

Above In Norse mythology, the Universe was divided into nine different worlds linked by the World Tree, Yggdrasil. The world of the gods (Aesir) was known as Asgard, *while the Earth was known as* Midgard. *This was surrounded by the sea and by a gigantic serpent, the offspring of the trickster god, Loki. Here, Thor is shown fishing for the serpent, the symbol of evil. It escaped, however, when the giant Hymir (also shown right) cut the line.*

> "Flocks die, friends die, you yourself die likewise. But if one has won an honoured name, then that can never die."
>
> The *Havamal*

Ragnarok

Although the gods were thought to be superhuman they were not immortal, and Norse religion looked to the day of Ragnarok when the gods themselves would perish in battle. From this destruction would be born a new world, which would worship an almighty god. This belief was influenced by Christianity, which was spreading across Europe at that time.

The Celts

Little is known for certain about the religious practices of the Celts, who occupied large parts of western Europe including pre-Roman Britain, Ireland and northwestern France, in the Iron Age. What is known comes largely from Roman sources, which are inclined to interpret Celtic religion unfavourably. There is some evidence that they worshipped gods from other cultures, including Mercury and Mars, but they added local gods of their own.

Fertility cults

The figure of a naked male god wearing horns or antlers is a recurring symbol in Celtic mythology, as is the Earth Mother – both of whom are associated with fertility. The Celtic tribes treated the natural world as sacred – particularly wells, springs, lakes and rivers, which were seen as sources of life.

ZOROASTRIANISM

A lthough Zoroastrianism is an ancient faith, it is still a living religion practised by some 200,000 people living mainly in Iran and in India, where they are known as Parsees.

Zarathustra

Zoroastrianism is a monotheistic religion founded by the prophet Zarathustra, also known as Zoroaster. Although he is traditionally thought to have lived in the 6th century BCE, recent scholarship suggests he could have been born as long ago as 1200BCE. Little is known for certain of his early life in what is now northeast Iran, but it is believed that he was inspired to teach and spread the faith after receiving a series of visions from the Supreme God, Ahura Mazda, at the age of 30. After his death many legends grew up describing him as a magician, an astrologer, a mathematician and a philosopher, but it is likely that in his lifetime he was a practising priest within the Aryan tradition, which used the household fire as the focus of a belief system and drew on the power of the natural elements of rain, wind and Sun.

Above This relief shows griffins, which are sacred mythological creatures – half-man and half-animal. They are traditionally found on doorposts and gateways to protect against evil.

Good and evil

Zarathustra developed a religion based on the coming of a saviour, the resurrection of the dead, and a day of judgement when wrongdoers will go to hell and the just will be rewarded in heaven. Much of his thinking has been absorbed by other faiths – in particular, by Judaism, Christianity and Islam.

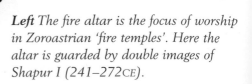

Left The fire altar is the focus of worship in Zoroastrian 'fire temples'. Here the altar is guarded by double images of Shapur I (241–272CE).

Above and below At the age of seven children are initiated into the faith and presented with the kusti, *the sacred cord that is wrapped three times round the waist over a white tunic. During prayers (five times daily), worshippers face a source of light and undo the* kusti.

Zarathustra taught that Ahura Mazda created life and all that was good but that he was locked in a struggle with Angra Mainyu, the Spirit of Evil, who would one day be destroyed by the forces of goodness.

Zoroastrianism stresses that individuals have free will to choose between good or evil and their deeds will be judged as they cross the Chinvat Bridge between life and death. For the righteous it is wide, but for the wicked it narrows to the width of a blade.

The magi

The Three Wise Men, who were the first non-Jews present shortly after Christ's birth and who gave gifts of gold, myrrh and frankincense, are believed by some to have been Zoroastrian priests, or magi. Today, the magi carry out worship in 'fire temples'. The sacred fire represents the purity of God, source of light and life.

21

AZTEC AND INCA BELIEFS

Before the arrival of Christopher Columbus from Spain in 1492, Central America had a history of Amerindian (American Indian) culture stretching back to the 12th century BCE. The Aztecs and the Incas represent the high point of that civilization, which was destroyed by Spanish invaders in the 16th century CE.

Left *Quetzalcoatl was the Aztec god of learning and priesthood. He is often depicted as a plumed serpent.*

The Aztecs

The Aztecs believed that the Universe was made up of different levels. At the bottom was the underworld: a cold, dark, inhospitable realm reserved for those who did not go to paradise. At the top were two heavenly beings who had created humanity. In between was the Earth. The forces of heaven and the underworld came together at the Great Temple in Tenochtitlan, the Aztec capital.

Worship of the Sun

The most important element in the Aztecs' lives was the Sun, which was believed to be a warrior god constantly engaged in battle with the forces of darkness. Only if the Sun god Huitzilopochtli remained strong would the world and the Aztec civilization survive. Human sacrifice (usually of enemy warriors captured in battle) became a central feature of their religious practices because they believed they had to feed the Sun god with blood every day. Victims were held down alive on an altar while a priest used a sharp stone knife to cut out the still-beating heart. Then the heart and the blood were offered to the god who, now he was fed, would continue to protect them. Every year thousands of people lost their lives in this way. When Aztec warriors died, they were thought to join the Sun for four years before returning to Earth as hummingbirds.

Below *The double-headed serpent was one of the symbols of Tlaloc, the rain god. The serpent was worn as an ornament by the high priests.*

Right The fortified Inca city of Machu Picchu, high in the Andes mountains of Peru, was never discovered by the Spanish invaders. It contains a temple for worship of the Sun.

Below A couple dress as emperor and empress during a modern-day re-creation of the Inti-Raymi Festival, held on 21 June (the winter solstice) in Cuzco, Peru. This great festival of Inti, the Sun god, lasts for nine days, with sacrifices, feasting and dancing.

The Incas

The Incas first settled in the Cuzco region of the Andes in present-day Peru around the 13th century CE. They believed that certain places or objects possessed a supernatural power. These could be mountains, rivers, buildings or ancient shrines and were known as *huacas*. The *huacas* were treated with great reverence and became key elements in what Incas believed was a sacred landscape centred on their capital Cuzco.

The Inca gods

The Incas' main god was Viracocha, the creator of all things, who was believed to have made the Sun, the Moon, and all humanity. Alongside him were Inti, the Sun god, and Illapa, the weather god. As with the Aztecs, worship of the Sun was very important because it was the source of life, ripening crops and bringing heat and light.

At times of crisis human sacrifice was carried out, but usually the sacrifices involved killing a llama or offering maize beer. Ancestor worship was very important in Inca life and, like the Egyptians, they practised the art of mummification, which meant embalming their dead and treating them as sacred objects. The Incas believed that after death good people joined the Sun in heaven and revealed themselves on Earth as *huacas*.

TRADITIONAL BELIEFS: AN INTRODUCTION

Unlike the global missionary religions of Christianity and Islam, which have been exported far beyond their place of origin in the Middle East, and unlike the Jewish faith, which is practised by adherents all over the world, traditional religions survive in remote areas among comparatively small communities or tribes.

Below This North American totem pole, richly carved with gods and goddesses, reflects the creation stories that are passed down the generations.

The natural world

It is misleading to refer to tribal peoples as primitive, because although in the past they lived in the less advanced parts of the world and lacked modern technology, they developed elaborate societies with ritual practices that suggest they are far more religious than many other peoples. Tribal peoples live close to the natural world on which they rely for food and shelter. They have an instinctive understanding of the fragility of life and realize that they are at the mercy of the elements. Consequently, they look to forces greater than themselves for protection and help in times of uncertainty or danger.

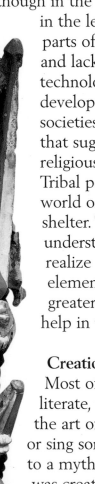

Creation stories

Most of these tribal societies are non-literate, that is to say, they do not practise the art of writing. Instead they tell stories or sing songs, which often take them back to a mythological time when the Earth was created. They tell stories of gods and goddesses who grow angry if they are not treated with proper respect and who reward those who carry out their religious duties properly. These creation stories are part of a tribe's spiritual heritage and are passed down by word of mouth, from generation to generation.

"Behold this buffalo, O Grandfather, which you have given us. From him the people live and with him they walk the sacred path."

Sioux Indian prayer

Left This mask belongs to the Yoruba people of Nigeria. Aspects of a god's spiritual power are thought to be passed on to the wearer of the mask.

Above *The creation stories of the Aboriginals are re-enacted in rituals of song and dance known as* corroborees. *They recall the Dreamtime, when fantastic creatures roamed the Earth and left their mark on the landscape.*

The spirit world

As well as a creator god, there are believed to be many more individual spirits whose help can be sought in everyday life. These may be associated with special places (for example, a clearing in the forest or a particular rock), or with tribal activities (hunting, pot-making or farming). The spirit world is divided into good and evil. Evil spirits, associated with witches and demons, are thought to bring about disasters for the tribe (a failed harvest, a drought or defeat by an enemy) and for individuals (sickness or the death of a child). At such times the people turn to shaman, who possesses powers to counteract the evil spirits and to return people to health.

Respect for the gods also mirrors respect for parents. Boys and girls are expected to show reverence towards their elders and care for them in old age. An Akan proverb from Ghana says, "If your parents take care of you up to the time you cut your teeth, you take care of them when they lose theirs."

ABORIGINAL AND MAORI BELIEFS

To the Aboriginal people of Australia, the land is a sacred place criss-crossed by energy and unseen spiritual forces. For them the spirit world is inseparable from the natural world, and elements of the landscape such as mountains, trees and water-holes are treated as holy sites.

The Dreamtime

The landscape is believed to have come into being at a distant time in history known as the Dreamtime. At that time fantastic beings, half-human and half-animal, peopled the world. They left their mark (literally) on the Earth so that a footprint became a valley, for example, or a thumb-print a lake. Aboriginals believe that these beings are their distant ancestors. Each person is believed to have been born with his or her own Dreaming, so that someone with, say, a Honey Ant Dreaming can point to a honey ant and say, "This is my great-great-great-great grandfather."

Above *Aboriginals look back to their ancestral past, which they believe was populated by fantastic creatures, and believe that they are directly related to elements of the natural world. This modern painting is of a Snake Dreaming.*

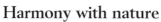

Harmony with nature

Stories from the Dreamtime are passed on down the generations, depicted on bark paintings and re-enacted in dance, song and ritual. The spirits of the Ancestors are everywhere, in the land (*manta*) and in people (*anangu*). The traditional life of the Aboriginal is lived close to the natural world and they are taught, according to the Laws of the Dreamtime, to treat it with great respect. In return, they will have nothing to fear from it.

Left *This bark painting depicts a Wandjina – an ancestral being from the sea and sky that brings rain and controls the fertility of the land and the animals.*

Left *Maoris greet each other by pressing their noses together in a* hongi. *It is a symbol of welcome and friendship.*

The Aboriginals killed only what they needed to eat and developed such a close understanding of the natural environment that they could follow the tracks of a kangaroo over huge distances. Breaking Laws of the Dreamtime would, they believed, bring catastrophe, and losing their land would be like losing their souls. This is what many of them believe has happened today. White settlers who began colonizing the continent 300 years ago have gradually forced them off their ancestral lands into cities and reservations cut off from their historic past.

The Maoris

In the beginning, according to Maori tradition, Sky Father and Earth Mother held each other in darkness in a deep embrace. Between them lay their children – the gods of wind, forest, sea and food, and a god known as 'the fierce one'. To reach the light the children had to force their parents apart, which the forest god Tane did by putting his head on his mother and his feet on his father and pushing hard. This separation was necessary for humanity but it was also sad, and that sadness is expressed in the raindrops, which fall like tears from the sky.

Although their creation stories differ from those of the Aboriginals, the Maoris, who came to Aotearoa (New Zealand) from an ancient homeland called Hawaiki in around 750BCE, share with them a communal life based on respect for the land. At the birth of a child the father or priest recites a prayer, or *karakia*, an appeal to the gods for special power. At death it is believed the spirit will return to the ancestral homeland.

Below The Maori meeting-house, richly carved with scenes from the past, is part of communal life. The foreground of the meeting-house is sacred and it is here that bodies are brought before burial.

NATIVE AMERICANS

When the first European settlers arrived in the 16th century they came into contact with Native Americans who were not one nation but members of many different tribes scattered throughout North America. While some elements of their religions overlapped, there were many differences in their religious rituals.

The Great Spirit

Many Native Americans believe that the world has been created by a Great Spirit and that there are other spiritual powers all around them, usually in the form of the natural landscape, which they consider sacred. This Great Spirit has many names: for the Sioux Indians it is Wakan Tanka, for the Hopi it is Masau, for the Iroquois it is Orenda, and for the Ojibwa it is Kitche Manitou.

Creation myths

Native Americans have elaborate creation myths that they tell to their children and re-enact in ritual dances. The Iroquois, for example, believe that, before the Earth was made, everyone lived in the sky. When the Sky Chief's daughter fell through a hole into the waters below she was rescued by two swans. At her request other animals took it in turns to dive into the waves, until eventually a toad dived down and returned to the surface with a mouthful of soil. The toad spat it out onto the shell of a turtle and from this the Earth grew.

Right A medicine mask dance is performed by the Indians of the northeast (today's Ontario) to invoke the powers of the spirit world for healing purposes.

Guardian spirits

In addition to the creator gods, Native Americans look to guardian spirits which, if treated with respect and given presents of food and tobacco, will take care of them and bless them with strength, health and a long life. They also believe in evil spirits which have to be fought or avoided. The Navajo and the Apache have a particular dread of ghosts, which they think could cause them harm. The medicine man is an important figure in the tribe. He is a shaman, a priest and a healer, and is thought to have close contact with the spirit world.

Close to nature

Some early Native Americans settled down and established agricultural communities while others were nomadic hunters wandering from place to place, but all of them were influenced by the cycle of the seasons. At key moments in the year – the migration of the buffalo, the return of fish upstream from the sea or the ripening of the maize and tobacco crops – they would offer up prayers of thanksgiving.

Above The hunters of the plains had a very special relationship with the buffalo on which they relied for food and clothing. The Plains Indians killed only what they needed and in some tribes asked the animal's pardon through prayer before killing it.

Right A revelation mask, made by the Kwakiutl Indian tribe from the northwest, opens up to reveal a second mask. These masks portray trickster gods, who show the tribe that the world is not always as it may seem.

Fighting for survival

Native Americans suffered the same fate as the Aboriginals of Australia when they were invaded and their traditional homelands were overrun. The United States authorities once tried to ban certain religious rituals (particularly the use of the hallucinogenic cactus, peyote, which was believed to bring closer contact with the spirit world). Recently they have supported the Native American beliefs, which themselves have influenced some New Age beliefs.

AFRICAN RELIGION

It is thought that about 15 per cent of the African population practises some form of local or native religion alongside the continent's most widespread religions, Christianity and Islam.

Creation stories

Creation stories vary from tribe to tribe. The Dinka people of southern Sudan tell of a woman who accidentally pierced a hole in the sky while she was hoeing the ground. The sky god was angry and sent disease and death through the tear she had made. From that moment suffering entered the world. The Barotse people of Zambia have a different story. They tell of a time when the creator, Nyambi, lived happily on Earth with his wife, Nasilele, and the human beings he had created. Their leader, Kamonu, was an ambitious man who annoyed the gods so much with his naughty ways that they decided to leave him and the Earth behind. Nyambi sought the help of a giant spider, which wove a web up to the heavens.

As Nyambi and Nasilele escaped they were followed by Kamonu, who had built a wooden tower. This crashed to the ground, leaving Kamonu stranded on Earth, able to see the gods only in the form of the Sun and the Moon.

Other gods

African tribes have a strong sense of an unseen spirit world behind the everyday world they can see, touch, hear and smell. The link between these two worlds is the shaman, or witch doctor. As well as practising traditional medicine, the people believe that he can travel through the spirit world while in a trance.

Above *Eshu, the trickster god of Nigeria, is depicted on batik. As in Native American belief, these spirits of mischief demonstrate that the world is not a predictable place but has many surprises to offer.*

Left *In the Juju dance of Cameroon, dancers dressed as forest spirits tell the story of the destruction of the forests and the natural environment.*

Right *In some parts of West Africa men have their own stool, which is elaborately carved and is said to contain part of the man's spirit. The men often carry their stools to tribal meetings.*

There are also a number of so-called 'trickster gods', who do strange and unexpected things to show that, although there is order in the Universe, there is also chaos and mystery.

The gods are usually at the service of a supreme god, who has a variety of names. It is Amma for the Dogon tribe in Mali, Chukwu for the Igbo of Nigeria, and Vidye Mukulu for the Baluba of the Democratic Republic of Congo (formerly Zaire).

Above *In Zambia, a* ng'anga, *or shaman, treats a patient. It is believed that some illnesses are caused by a breakdown in relationships between humanity and the natural world. The* ng'anga *tries to restore that balance by calling on higher powers.*

Community life

A sense of community and co-operation is vital to tribal African societies. Their world is a network of interdependent relationships, in which the strong help the weak, the young protect the old, and the elders instruct the children. This is summed up in the African proverb, "It takes a village to raise a child." Young men and women are expected to get married soon after initiation into adulthood. It is extremely rare for someone not to marry. They are also expected to have children so that they can fulfil their spiritual obligations to become an ancestor. The spirits of the dead are thought to live on and visit the Earth. Small wooden cages are sometimes found outside homes where a spirit can stay during these visits.

HINDUISM: AN INTRODUCTION

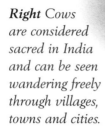

The origin of the word Hindu is to be found in the word *Sindhu*, which refers to the River Indus to the northwest of India in modern-day Pakistan. Hinduism is inextricably linked to the land of India itself and has come to mean that cluster of religious beliefs and practices that has grown up over the past 4,500 years on the Indian subcontinent.

The word Hinduism is a modern one that came into being as recently as the 19th century. Hindus themselves refer to their religion in a number of different ways (*see* page 44). One of these is *dharma*, a Sanskrit word with two meanings. The first is the cosmic law by which all creation is governed; and the second is appropriate conduct, or the proper way of behaving to achieve one's spiritual goals.

Right Cows are considered sacred in India and can be seen wandering freely through villages, towns and cities.

Hinduism was born out of one of the world's oldest civilizations, but unlike other religions it has no single founder, prophet or messenger. Instead, it represents a gradual development of thought, philosophy and devotion. It is not a creed (with rules and set beliefs), but a way of life that seeks to free believers from worldly attachments so that they can appreciate what is true and eternal.

Although eight out of ten people in India (which has a population of around 900 million) describe themselves as Hindu, their approach to the religion, and the way in which they practise it, varies from region to region.

Right A flowing river is a living symbol for Hindus, who see human life as an ongoing cycle from the source of the river to the sea, and back again to the source. Here at Varanasi, pilgrims bathe in the Ganges River as part of their religious devotions.

The belief in reincarnation

The different Hindu traditions are all linked by common threads. One of these is a belief in reincarnation – that when people die they are born again into a new life somewhere in the material world, their new identity (or incarnation) dictated by the good (or bad) deeds they have done while alive. This belief in the ongoing cycle of life, from birth to death to rebirth, is contained in the word *samsara*. The spiritual goal of Hindus is to purify themselves in each successive life so that eventually they will achieve *moksha* – release from the cycle of time, and deliverance into the ultimate reality of eternity itself. This eternity is known as *Brahman*, the godhead (source and origin of all creation).

During the early period of its development, Hindu society was divided into four classes (*varnas*). At the top were the *Brahmins*, who were learned in the scriptures and were permitted to become priests. Beneath them were the *Kshatriyas*, or warrior class, followed by the tradesmen and farmers, known as *Vaishyas*. Last came the *Shudras*, or labourers and servants. Today, the Indian government is trying to improve the lives of the lowest group, the *Dalit* ('the oppressed'). Sometimes known as the 'untouchables', they usually do the most menial work. But attitudes towards many of these people are still largely negative. The hardship of their life is made bearable by the belief that in a future incarnation they may climb higher up the spiritual ladder.

THE HOLY MEN

Sadhus, or Hindu holy men, lead an ascetic life. They practise self-discipline and avoid all sensual pleasure in order to develop greater spiritual powers. They have a solitary life, wandering from place to place and begging for just enough to survive. They also wear very few clothes (some wear no clothing at all) and sometimes perform acts of extreme penance such as prolonged fasting or living alone in remote mountain caves during the winter. Ordinary Indian men and women respect the *sadhus'* chosen way of life and will often ask them for advice on how best to lead their own lives. Their dramatic appearance is accepted as a completely normal feature of Indian life. The spiritual is an inseparable part of everyday life for most of the Indian population.

THE ORIGINS OF HINDUISM

Hinduism has its origins in the civilization that developed some 4,500 years ago along the Indus Valley, a corridor of fertile land stretching from the Himalayas through present-day Pakistan to the Arabian Sea. This civilization flourished from c.2500–1500BCE, and produced a highly developed culture centred on two cities: Mohenjo-Daro and Harappa.

Early history

Archaeological excavations made in 1921 revealed that these cities, the first on the Indian subcontinent, were enormous in size and elaborate in construction. The streets were laid out in a grid pattern and the buildings were solid with high defences. What also came to light were numerous clay figurines depicting a mother goddess. She seems to have been worshipped as a source of life and creation and is a forerunner of the mother goddess Mahadevi in classical Hinduism.

The Vedic period

Some scholars claim that around 1500BCE tribes of Aryan people from the Caucasus region of Central Asia invaded the Indus Valley and the northwest plains of the Indian subcontinent. They brought with them their traditions and their language (which later became Sanskrit) and mixed elements of their own culture with the existing culture of the Indus Valley. Others say that it was development within the tradition, not invasion by an outside force, that brought about changes to the religion.

Left This terracotta model from Mohenjo-Daro may be of the Mother Goddess who represented life, fertility and the fruits of the Earth. She was worshipped as someone who provided and cared for humankind.

A typical Harrapan house had an open courtyard. Thick windowless walls kept the inside of the house cool.

The brick-built houses, many with grain stores, had a sophisticated drainage system.

Below At its peak, Mohenjo-Daro had a population of around 30,000. Many of the buildings were made of baked brick – and the bricks were made to a uniform size.

The public bathing house may have been used for ritual purification.

Below This model chariot with bullocks was found in Harappa. Such artefacts suggest that this was an increasingly sophisticated civilization that recognized a connection between the natural and the spiritual worlds.

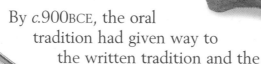

By *c.*900BCE, the oral tradition had given way to the written tradition and the religious beliefs were put into writing in the form of the sacred texts we know as the four *Vedas* (*see* page 38). The Vedic religion that developed in this period is based on the ritual sacrifice of animals to many different gods, especially Indra, the god of war and storms, and Agni, the god of fire. Vedic religion has much in common with ancient Greek and Roman gods, who also represent the elements and the forces of nature.

The *Puranas*

In the early centuries of the Common Era (CE), religious ideas and practices crystallized into the kind of Hinduism broadly recognized today. During this period the completion of the epic poems the *Mahabharata* and the *Ramayana* marked a cultural and religious step forward. Creation stories and stories about the lives of the gods appeared in another collection of sacred texts, known as the *Puranas* (*see* pages 38–39). Rules were eventually drawn up to govern the way that Hindus should lead their lives. These included four stages, or *ashramas*, which Hindus should ideally experience if they are to reach *moksha* – liberation from the ongoing cycle of birth, death and rebirth. The four stages are: being a student to learn about the sacred literature; being a householder to develop responsibility in society; being a contemplative to reflect and meditate on important things in life; and being an ascetic and to renounce the pleasures of the world.

HINDU GODS AND GODDESSES

Hindus believe in one god as the ultimate source of reality and existence. They describe their god as Brahman, the unseen, all-powerful force responsible for bringing all creation into being, and to which all creation will ultimately return. Brahman is neutral and impersonal and has to be approached through a series of personal deities, both male and female. The principal deities are Brahma, Vishnu, Shiva and the goddess Mahadevi, but there are many more gods besides. These include gods from the Vedic period.

Below Ganesh, the Remover of Obstacles, is portrayed as a man with an elephant's head. Ganesh is often honoured at the start of a journey. He is traditionally very fond of sweets and most statues to him show him holding some sweets in his hand.

Right Hanuman is the clever monkey god who came to the aid of Rama when he was fighting the demon, Ravana, King of Lanka. Hanuman is worshipped as a source of protection.

The deities from this period represent the forces of nature and include chiefly Agni, Indra and Varuna. Agni is the god of fire, and the life force of nature. Varuna is one of the chief Vedic gods. He maintains the cosmic order, has the power to punish and reward and is worshipped as god of the waters and oceans. These gods are addressed in the thousand or so hymns which make up the sacred text known as the *Rig Veda* (*see* page 38).

In addition to the chief gods, there are lesser gods such as Vayu, the god of wind, and Surya, the god of the Sun. Hindus believe that there are elements of the divine in all living things, so particular animals are worshipped as part of the divine plan. In four of his incarnations the god Vishnu assumes the form of an animal. He appears as a fish, a tortoise, a boar and a man-lion.

Two other gods who have a particular importance in Hindu worship are Hanuman, the monkey god, and Ganesh, one of the two sons of Shiva. Ganesh is a very popular god in India. It is said that following a misunderstanding Ganesh's father, Shiva, accidentally beheaded him. When he realized his mistake he was so upset that he promised to replace his head with the head of the first living thing he saw – which happened to be an elephant. Ganesh, who is known as the Remover of Obstacles and is worshipped as the god of learning, is portrayed with a human body (and a large pot belly!) and an elephant's head with one tusk. Hindus often have a favourite deity and may have a special shrine in the home.

Right Indra is the sky god and the god of rain. He is often portrayed wearing a turban or a fiery tiara. He sits astride an elephant and speeds across the sky.

THE SACRED WRITINGS

The earliest of the Hindu scriptures are the four texts known collectively as the *Vedas*, which were begun before 1000BCE. They are the first examples of Hindu written tradition. The oldest of the *Vedas* is the *Rig Veda*, which contains more than 1,000 hymns written in Sanskrit and is addressed to the elemental gods of fire, earth, air and water.

Much later, an important collection of philosophical works known as the *Upanishads* appeared. These try to explain the meaning of existence and to provide answers to the big questions in life, such as where we come from, why we are here and what will happen to us when we die. The *Vedas* and the *Upanishads* are regarded as the revealed words of God and not a single syllable of them can be changed. In addition to a collection known as the *Puranas*, which contains stories of the lives and adventures of the gods, there are two other important works of Hindu literature, called the *Mahabharata* and the *Ramayana*.

Above *A chariot fight takes place between Bhima and Arjuna, two Pandava brothers, and Drona, leader of the opposing forces.*

The *Mahabharata*
The *Mahabharata* was written in its present form in the third or second century BCE and is probably the largest single poem in the world, containing about 200,000 lines. This epic poem tells the story of the war between the five Pandava brothers, helped by their distant relative Krishna, and their 100 cousins, who live in Kurukshetra, near modern Delhi. The war, caused by a dispute over who is the rightful ruler, is long and bitter. Although the five brothers eventually win, the story gains its power from the different attitudes shown by the brothers to the realities of fighting. The third brother, called Arjuna, is a superb fighter and commander but objects to warfare. As the story unfolds, the reader is presented with discussions about every aspect of Hindu life, including its laws, politics, geography, astronomy and science. Consequently, what emerges alongside an exciting story of warfare is a kind of textbook of Hindu thinking.

"These words of glory to the God who is light shall be words supreme among things that are great. I glorify Varuna almighty, the god who is loving towards him who adores. We praise you with our thoughts, O God. We praise you as the Sun praises you in the morning; may we find joy in being your servants."

Extract from the *Rig Veda* in honour of Varuna, the upholder of the cosmic order

Above The Ramayana *is more than 50,000 lines long, and was written down around 200BCE. It tells the adventures of Prince Rama of Ayodhya, seen here sitting with his brothers and companions, having rescued his wife Sita from the clutches of Ravana, the ten-headed demon king of Lanka.*

Right Om is the sacred word for god and is repeated in mantra or prayers. Its deep humming sound is supposed to be a living contact with the divine presence.

The Bhagavad Gita

A central section of the *Mahabharata* is known as the Bhagavad Gita (the Song of the Lord). It is a conversation between Arjuna and his charioteer (who is none other than Krishna, the incarnation of Vishnu), but it also explores the essential questions of life. It is a meditation on the nature of God and an exploration of the ways of achieving liberation (*moksha*) through work, devotion and knowledge. If the *Mahabharata* is sometimes described as an encyclopaedia of Hindu life, the 18 chapters that make up the Bhagavad Gita are often regarded as the 'bible' of Hinduism.

THE HINDU TRINITY

The Hindu idea of God is contained in the word *Brahman*, which means 'the origin and the cause of all existence'. Brahman appears to humans in various forms and is worshipped in the shape of different gods and goddesses. Chief among these are three male gods: Brahma, Vishnu and Shiva – the Hindu Trinity. Brahma is the creator who brings the Universe into existence; Vishnu preserves life and all living things; Shiva is the destroyer (also known as the Lord of Time) who destroys the world. This ongoing cycle of creation, preservation and destruction is at the centre of Hindu belief. There is no real end or beginning to life. The beginning is an end and the end is a new beginning.

Above Brahma sits upon the lotus from which he was born at the time of creation. His wife is Sarasvati, the goddess of learning.

Brahma the creator

Since Brahma is the lord of all creation, he is considered to be above human worship and very few temples are dedicated to him. When he is shown in paintings and carvings, he is often seen with four faces and four arms, and sometimes on a swan or a lotus flower.

Above A group of young Indian women pray in front of a shrine representing the Hindu mother goddess, Mahadevi.

Vishnu the preserver

Vishnu is responsible for controlling human fate. He appears in ten incarnations, or *avatars*. The two most important are Krishna, the most popular god, and Rama. Vishnu is often portrayed riding majestically across the heavens on an eagle (Garuda). In his hand he may hold a discus, symbolizing the Sun, or a mace, suggesting the power of nature.

Below Shiva the destroyer dances in a circle of fire. At his feet lies a demon he has killed.

Matsya the fish saved humanity from the flood.

Kurma the turtle carried the world on his back.

Varaha the boar raised the Earth with his tusks.

Narasimha, half-man and half-lion, defeated evil demons.

Vamana the dwarf defeated demons.

Rama fights against evil in the world and upholds virtue and law.

Krishna is renowned as a warrior, a teacher and a lover.

Parasurama (Rama with an axe) defeated the warrior caste.

Kalki, who will appear riding a white horse, is yet to come.

Buddha is 'the enlightened one' and the founder of Buddhism.

Above The protective power of Vishnu (shown in the centre of the picture in the form of Krishna with his consort Radha) appears on Earth in ten incarnations, or avatars, which prevent evil in the world.

Shiva the destroyer

Shiva is a god in whom all opposites meet and are resolved into one. So, while Shiva is believed to be responsible for destroying creation, he is also thought to be responsible for re-creating it. Shiva's wife appears in many forms, each representing an aspect of his character. Kali is fierce, and is depicted surrounded by skulls or carrying severed heads and limbs. Parvati is known for her kindness and gentleness, and is often shown with her son Ganesh, who has an elephant's head and one tusk.

HINDU WORSHIP

Daily worship is known as *puja* and for most Hindus is usually carried out in the home. A shrine richly decorated with pictures or statues (*murtis*) of favourite gods is set aside for this purpose. Wealthier families sometimes set aside a whole room as a shrine and worship there individually or as a family. *Puja* begins with the simplest but most important prayer (*mantra*) – the saying of the sacred word *Om* to make contact with the divine. This is followed by the recitation of other mantras from the scriptures and the offering of gifts (sweets, money, fruit, etc.) to a particular god.

Worship is also carried out in the temple (*mandir*) under the supervision of a *Brahmin*, or high caste priest. Although Hindus believe that their god is everywhere, they also believe that the temple is his special home. Only the priest is allowed to come close to the divine presence which 'resides' in the inner sanctuary of the building, in the holy of holies known as the *garbhagriha* (womb-house).

Above *Children light candles to celebrate Diwali, the festival of lights.*

Below *Women pray in a Hindu temple on the Indonesian island of Bali.*

Before worship begins, members of the congregation carry out elaborate rituals of purification, which may involve washing the feet, rinsing the mouth or preparing special food. The priest leads the worship by reading from the sacred texts and saying mantras. Small devotional lamps (*divas*) are lit, and after worship, the people share the food that has been blessed and offered to the gods.

Making a pilgrimage

Pilgrimage is an important part of Hindu worship and involves making the effort to travel to a sacred site. As such, it is considered an act of worship in itself. Particularly holy are sites associated with the birth or life of a god, such as Ayodhya, the legendary birthplace of Lord Rama; Kurukshetra, where the great war described in the *Mahabharata* is said to have taken place; Varanasi, also known as 'the city of light' and believed to be the home of Lord Shiva; and Mathura, the birthplace of Lord Krishna. In addition, many Hindus will make a special journey to fords, or safe crossing places in rivers, which symbolize the crossing from one life to another and the transition from *samsara* to *moksha* (*see* page 33) which every devout Hindu hopes to make. The most sacred river in India is the Ganges, named after Ganga, the river goddess. Bathing in its waters is an act of devotion, and bathing at the pilgrimage site of Varanasi is thought to be particularly special.

> "Lights are lit in Hindu households to guide Lakshmi, the goddess of fortune, into the home."
>
> From the *Mahabharata*

Above The Dusserah festival takes place in September or October. Effigies are burnt in a re-enactment of the triumph of Rama, Lakshman and Hanuman over the demon Ravana, recorded in the epic Ramayana.

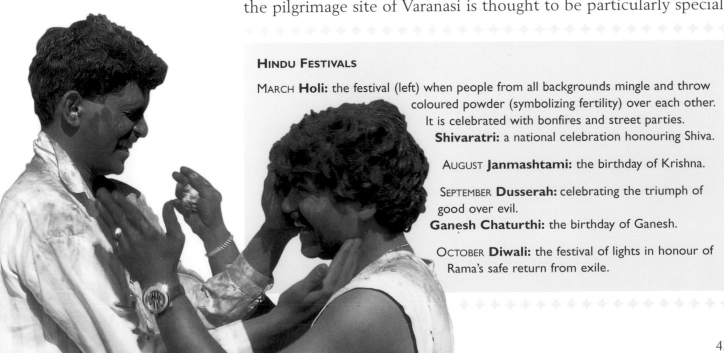

HINDU FESTIVALS

MARCH **Holi:** the festival (left) when people from all backgrounds mingle and throw coloured powder (symbolizing fertility) over each other. It is celebrated with bonfires and street parties.
Shivaratri: a national celebration honouring Shiva.

AUGUST **Janmashtami:** the birthday of Krishna.

SEPTEMBER **Dusserah:** celebrating the triumph of good over evil.
Ganesh Chaturthi: the birthday of Ganesh.

OCTOBER **Diwali:** the festival of lights in honour of Rama's safe return from exile.

SOME HINDU BELIEFS

The word Hinduism was coined comparatively recently. It was introduced in the 19th century to describe a cluster of ancient Indian beliefs and religious practices. Hindus themselves are more inclined to refer to Hinduism by other names – *Dharma*, *Sanatana Dharma* (everlasting *Dharma*) or *Varnashramadharma*. These need some explanation because each word describes, in an Indian way, what people living in the West understand by Hinduism.

The four aims in life

Traditional Hinduism says that there are four aims in life. *Dharma*, the first aim, is the performance of duties appropriate to one's position in life. It also involves living a good life by being kind to others, telling the truth, helping one's neighbour, loving humanity and being prepared to make sacrifices for other people. Everlasting *Dharma* – *Sanatana Dharma* – stresses this idea. The second aim of Hindu life is *artha*, the achievement of material prosperity or the pursuit of legitimate worldly success. The third is *kama*, the enjoyment of legitimate pleasure. And the fourth is *moksha*, the ultimate release from attachment to the world.

Above This is one of 12 great wheels (symbolizing samsara, *or the wheel of life), intricately carved in stone on the temple of Surya the Sun god at Konaraka, on the east coast of India.*

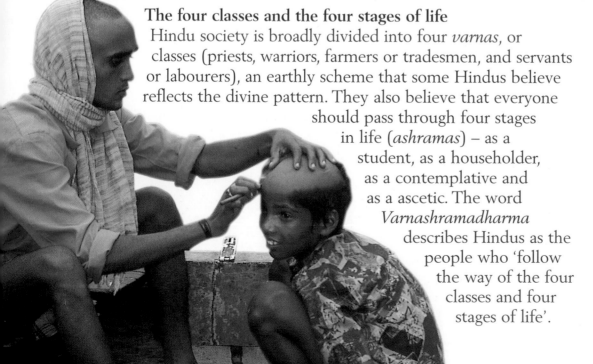

The four classes and the four stages of life

Hindu society is broadly divided into four *varnas*, or classes (priests, warriors, farmers or tradesmen, and servants or labourers), an earthly scheme that some Hindus believe reflects the divine pattern. They also believe that everyone should pass through four stages in life (*ashramas*) – as a student, as a householder, as a contemplative and as a ascetic. The word *Varnashramadharma* describes Hindus as the people who 'follow the way of the four classes and four stages of life'.

Left Between the ages of one and three, boys have their heads ritually shaved. This marks, in a formal way, a stage of development in life.

Above Ritual is very important in Hindu worship and practice. Here a couple exchange vows before committing themselves to marriage.

> "... the end of wisdom is Brahman, beginningless, supreme ... he sees all, he hears all. He is in all, and he is."
>
> Bhagavad Gita 13:12–13

The four stages are the spiritual milestones in a Hindu's time on earth. The role of student is crucial as it stresses the importance of education and the acquisition of knowledge to achieve enlightenment. The role of the householder underlines the importance of the family unit in Indian life. Hindus should then withdraw from the world as contemplatives, before becoming ascetics and cutting themselves off completely in preparation for death. This pattern is not rigidly followed by everyone, but it remains a powerful ideal for Hindus.

Birth and reincarnation

Each individual is believed to have an eternal soul (*atman*), which can be born millions of times into millions of forms or incarnations. The law of *karma* dictates how many times and how many forms. *Karma* is the moral law of the Universe, the cosmic principle by which the world and all living things operate. Good deeds done in this life ensure progress in the next. Life is an ongoing cycle of birth, death and rebirth (*samsara*). When people die, the soul leaves the body but is reborn into another body (human or animal). The precise nature of this new identity, or reincarnation, is determined by how well or badly a person has acted in previous lives. This process of reincarnation ends only when Hindus have achieved release (*moksha*) from *samsara* by freeing themselves from all attachments to worldly pleasure. Then the soul returns to the eternal stillness of the divine *Brahman*, or godhead.

JAINISM: AN INTRODUCTION

The guiding principle of Jainism is respect for life and all living things. Tradition says that the religion was founded in the 5th century BCE by Mahavira (the Great Hero) in the Ganges basin in northeast India. Like the Buddha, who was a contemporary, Mahavira was born into a high caste family, but at the age of 29 he renounced his wealth to live as a wandering beggar. Tired of the ongoing cycle of birth, death and rebirth and dissatisfied with the prevailing religious teachings, he set out to find enlightenment for

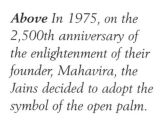

himself through practices that were increasingly ascetic (without material comforts). It is said that his first act was to tear out all his hair before leaving home. After 12 years of wandering he achieved perfect knowledge (*kevala*) through fasting and meditation. Once he had attained enlightenment, Mahavira gathered a small group of followers around him and taught and preached for the next 30 years before starving himself to death at the village of Pava, near to where he was born. Pava is still an important pilgrimage site for Jain followers.

Above In 1975, on the 2,500th anniversary of the enlightenment of their founder, Mahavira, the Jains decided to adopt the symbol of the open palm.

The *Jinas*

Jains take their name from the word *Jina* – someone who has conquered attachment to the world and won victory of knowledge and enlightenment.

There are said to be 24 *Jinas* (also known as *Tirthankaras*, or 'ford-makers'), of whom Mahavira is the last. These are spiritual guides able 'to make a ford across the ocean of rebirth' to allow people to achieve release from the cycle of death and achieve liberation from rebirth.

Right Shvetambara monks and nuns wear masks to prevent them breathing in tiny insects and killing them.

Left Every 12 or 13 years, the head of the immense statue of Lord Bahubali is anointed with offerings (turmeric water in this case) during a festival. The statue, erected in 981 CE, towers over the Jain holy site of Sravanabegola in Karnataka State, India.

Below This is a Jain celebration near Jabalpur in India.

The Five Great Vows

In Jainism, monks and nuns take Five Great Vows (*Mahavratas*) to help them on their path towards enlightenment. These are: *ahimsa*: not to harm any living thing; *satya*: to speak the truth; *asteya*: not to steal; *brahmacharya*: to abstain from sexual activity; and *aparigraha*: to give up all worldly things and human attachments. The vow of non-violence or non-injury is central to Jainism, and novice monks are given a broom to sweep away living creatures so they do not tread on them accidentally and kill them.

Around the 1st century CE the religion split into two sects. The *Digambaras* (literally, 'sky clad') believed that their total renunciation of worldly possessions meant that they should renounce clothing and (for men, not women) go completely naked. The *Shvetambaras* ('white clad') believed that monks and nuns could wear simple white robes.

There are thought to be about four million Jains worldwide, most of whom live on the Indian subcontinent where they are members of the merchant, banking and business communities.

JAIN BELIEF AND WORSHIP

Jains do not believe in one god, nor do they pray to gods to help them. Instead, they rely on spiritual teachers to train them in meditation and self-discipline, which will enable them to be released from the prison of day-to-day existence into the joy of ultimate liberation. Ordinary Jains, as well as monks and nuns, practise asceticism (giving up material comforts) because they believe that only through controlling natural desires and appetites can a person be free of the material world. Central to this belief is the concept of *karma*, which is different from that of the Hindus and Buddhists (*see* pages 45 and 59). For Jains, *karma* is composed of fine particles that stick to the soul, like mud sticks to a shoe, gradually building up and weighing it down. Doing bad deeds creates heavy *karma*, which prevents the soul's liberation, but doing good deeds causes the *karma* to be washed away, eventually allowing the liberated soul (*siddha*) to rise up to the heights of the Universe where it can live forever in spiritual freedom.

Above *This typically ornate carving is from the 14th-century* CE *Jain temple of Chaumukha.*

Right *Jain temples are beautiful works of architecture, often richly decorated and carved to show reverence for the sacred images (pujas) of the Tirthankaras placed inside. This one is in the Indian state of Gujarat. Worship may involve quiet meditation or the repetition of a mantra (a word or syllable believed to possess spiritual power). The worshipper may also decorate an image with flowers or anoint it with special liquids.*

Sources of *karma*

Jains believe that the principal sources of *karma* are: attachment to possessions and the material things in life; the expression of anger, pride, deceit or greed; and false belief. The rejection of material things can be used to the advantage of others, and Jains are known for their charitable giving and the way they use their wealth to build temples, hospitals and schools. Jains are encouraged to strengthen their devotional life by setting aside 48 minutes every day in which to practise meditation and to live one complete day as a monk during the major festival at Pajjusana.

Below *Many Jains have a shrine in their homes for daily worship. They rise before dawn and invoke the Five Supreme Beings, who represent stages along the path to spiritual liberation.*

SIKHISM: AN INTRODUCTION

The Sikh religion was founded in the 15th century CE by Guru Nanak (*guru* means spiritual guide or teacher) in the area of modern-day Pakistan and northwest India known as Punjab. It was a time of tension between Hindus and Muslims. Guru Nanak believed such religious conflicts were harmful and gathered around him a small group of followers who, like him, were searching for an understanding of God uncluttered by ritual. "There is neither Hindu nor Muslim. So whose path shall I follow?" he wondered. And he concluded, "I shall follow the path of God."

Sikhs believe in one god whom they call *Satguru*, or true teacher. They believe God created the world and all things in it, but that God is not visible in Creation. As a result God's will has to be made known through wise and holy teachers, or gurus. Sikhism has ten human gurus (Guru Nanak and his nine successors) and a final guru in the form not of a person but of a book – the *Adi Granth* (literally, The First Book). This is a collection of the writings of the gurus and is honoured in the same way as the ten human gurus – hence its more usual name, the *Guru Granth Sahib*.

Guru Nanak founded a religion based on the simple desire to get close to God and to do God's will. He also believed that true love of God is impossible without love of humanity, so he taught that men and women should be kind to their neighbours and share the fruits of their labours. In the beginning, Guru Nanak and his disciples formed a close-knit community devoted to singing and meditating on the Divine Name (*Nam*). Guru Nanak's hymns live on in Sikh worship practised today.

Above As a mark of equality, Sikhs often eat communally in a shared dining room, or langar, *attached to the temple, or* gurdwara. The gurdwara *is also a community centre and a base for charitable work in the community.*

Above Today, most of the Sikh population live in the agricultural state of Punjab in northwest India and Pakistan.

Right Guru Nanak (1469–1539CE) was the founder of Sikhism and the first of the ten gurus, or teachers, of the faith. After a religious experience at the age of 30, he became a wandering preacher before eventually settling in Kartarpur (in modern-day Pakistan), where he built the first Sikh temple.

THE TEN GURUS

Above *Guru Gobind Singh is surrounded by his sons. He was the last of the living gurus, and is chiefly remembered for founding the Khalsa and for his decision to treat the Sikh holy scripture as if it were itself a living guru.*

The development of Sikhism is inseparable from the lives of the Ten Gurus who shaped the religion over the first two centuries of its existence. The religion was founded by Guru Nanak in the 15th century CE, when he began to attract a group of followers who wanted a simpler, purer form of devotion uncluttered by ritual. Originally, the group led an intensely spiritual life, meditating on the name of God and singing the devotional hymns Nanak had written. They lived a communal life and followed three basic rules: *kirt karo* (hard work); *nam japo* (worship of the Divine Name); and *vand cauko* (sharing the fruits of their labours).

A succession of gurus

Nanak's successor was Guru Angad (1504–1552), who is chiefly remembered for composing the Gurmukhi script in which the Punjabi language was written down for worship. The third guru was Amar Das (1479–1574), who founded the town of Goindval in Punjab where Sikhs gathered twice a year to renew friendships and to deepen their faith. The fourth guru, Guru Ram Das (1534–1581) moved the Sikh's spiritual centre from Goindval to what is now Amritsar. The fifth guru, Guru Arjan (1563–1606), was the son of Guru Ram Das, who built the Golden Temple. The Sikhs' next leader, Guru Hargobind (1595–1644) transformed the community (the *Panth*) into a more militant force. Guru Har Rai (1630–1661) was the seventh Guru. He was followed by Har Krishan (1656–64) and then by Guru Tegh Bahadur (1621–1675) and Guru Gobind Singh (1666–1708).

Left *This Sikh is being initiated into the Khalsa (community of the pure) in the distinctive uniform worn by Guru Gobind Singh. He carries a ceremonial sword symbolizing his willingness to defend the faith against outside aggression.*

Above Sikh elders transport the Guru Granth Sahib *to the temple where it is installed with great ceremony.*

The *Guru Granth Sahib*

Guru Gobind Singh, the tenth and last living guru, is regarded with almost as much veneration as the founder, Guru Nanak. He was responsible for two key developments that have shaped the Sikh identity to this day. The first was the foundation of the *Khalsa* – the community of 'pure' Sikhs, who were prepared to die for their faith. They are baptized with holy water (*amrit*), given the name *Singh* meaning 'lion' (female members were called *Kaur* meaning 'princess') and told to wear a distinctive uniform that marked them out as brave soldier-saints. His second innovation was to place authority over the Sikh community, not in the person of a living guru but in the Sikh holy scripture. From then on, it was known as the *Guru Granth Sahib*.

Left The Guru Granth Sahib, *also known as the* Adi Granth *(the First Book), is the Sikhs' holiest scripture.*

AMRITSAR

Amritsar is the Sikh holy city in the state of Punjab in northwest India and Pakistan. It is here that the Golden Temple was completed in 1601, by the fifth gurus, Guru Arjan. The Golden Temple, also known in Punjabi as the Harimandir Sahib (House of God) is Sikhism's holiest shrine. By day it houses the holy scripture, the *Guru Granth Sahib*. At night the scripture is stored in a nearby building, the Akal Takht. While the Golden Temple is devoted to worship, the Akal Takht, or seat of temporal power, is a kind of parliament and conference hall where political and social matters are discussed.

Daily worship at the Golden Temple starts at four o'clock in the morning – an hour before the *Guru Granth Sahib* is installed each day – and continues until midnight. Hymns (*kirtan*) from the scriptures are sung all day long and the temple attracts a constant stream of visitors and pilgrims. During the early 19th century the Temple's two upper stories were covered with gold leaf. The name by which it is known to foreigners, the Golden Temple, dates from this time.

Although it is a focal-point of worship, the Golden Temple is part of a much larger complex of guest houses, conference centres, dining-halls, watchtowers, cloisters and a museum. At the entrance to the Temple compound is a gateway called the Darshani Deorhi, above which are stored the golden spades that were used to dig the lake. In front of the gateway is a cardamon tree where a small shrine marks the spot where Guru Arjan is believed to have sat while he supervised the excavation of the pool.

> **"All creatures on their actions are judged in God's court, just and true."**
>
> *Guru Granth Sahib*

Left *Pictures of the Ten Sikh Gurus and other religious souvenirs are sold to the hundreds of thousands of visitors who make a pilgrimage to the Golden Temple each year.*

Left and below The Golden Temple, which by day houses the Sikh scripture, the Guru Granth Sahib, is Sikhism's holiest shrine. Visitors and pilgrims reach it by a 60-metre causeway built across the Lake of Immortality. Moving across the lake to the shrine is in itself a solemn act of worship.

The temple complex has been the scene of many conflicts throughout its history. In the 18th century, it witnessed frequent fighting between the Sikhs on the one hand and the Moghuls or the Afghans on the other. The latest conflict was in 1984, when Indian security forces stormed the Golden Temple and shot dead a Sikh activist, the leader of a movement for Sikh independence. In the fighting that followed, the Akal Takht was virtually destroyed and had to be rebuilt. Later the same year the Indian Prime Minister, Indira Gandhi, was assassinated in a retaliation that prompted a massacre of Sikhs and several years of fighting between the Indian authorities and Sikh separatists.

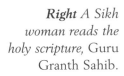

Right A Sikh woman reads the holy scripture, Guru Granth Sahib.

LIFE AS A SIKH

The turban is the most distinctive feature of Sikh dress but it is only one element of the traditional customs and practices of the faith. When a man is initiated into the Khalsa (becomes a full member of the Sikh religion), he must wear the Five Ks – so-called because the Punjabi words describing them each begin with a 'K'. They are: *kesh*, uncut hair covered by the turban; the *kirpan*, a short sword symbolizing resistance against evil; the *kara*, a steel bracelet symbolizing faithfulness to God (originally a protection for the sword arm); the *khanga*, a comb symbolizing personal hygiene; and the *kach*, knee-length breeches, symbolizing purity. Meat slaughtered in the Muslim way and tobacco and alcohol are forbidden, as are stealing, gambling and unfaithfulness to one's marriage partner. Sikhs should get up early, bathe, then meditate on the name of God (*Nam*). Each day they should read or recite from the scriptures and, if possible, join a congregation (*sangat*) at the temple (*gurdwara*) where they can listen to the words of the gurus and do charitable work.

At the centre of temple worship is the Sikh holy scripture, the *Guru Granth Sahib*. Members of the congregation must kneel in its presence and approach it barefoot and with the head covered. On special occasions a temple supervisor, or *Granthi*, may lead the worship, waving a type of fan or whisk (a *chauri*) over the text as he reads the words aloud. At the end of the recitation of hymns the congregation joins in the collective prayer (*ardas*).

Above At a Sikh wedding the bride often wears traditional Punjabi red. Gifts of money are made to the couple and passages from the Guru Granth Sahib are read out to bless the marriage.

Left This Sikh wears traditional costume demonstrating the Five Ks – kesh, kirpan, kara, khanga *and* kach.

Right *The Khanda is a sign often used for Sikhism. The central double-edged sword symbolizes belief in one god. The two outer blades represent spiritual and temporal power.*

The *Guru Granth Sahib* also plays a part in family ceremonies. For example, in the naming of newborn babies the book is opened at random and the first letter of the first hymn on that page is used as the first letter of the baby's name. At a marriage ceremony (*anand karaj*), the bride and groom walk round the holy book four times as a sign of its importance in their future life together. A section of the scripture known as the *Kirtan Sohila* is read at funeral services. The dead person is dressed in the traditional Five Ks and the body is cremated as soon as possible, usually on the day of death. To mark births, deaths and marriages, Sikhs often hold an "*akhand path*", a continuous 48-hour reading of the *Guru Granth Sahib* timed to end at dawn on the day of the particular event being celebrated. Sikh festivals (*gurpurbs*) usually commemorate the birth or death of one of the ten gurus or an event associated with his life.

Right *This young girl wears traditional costume at the festival for Guru Gobind Singh's birthday.*

SIKH FESTIVALS

DECEMBER/JANUARY Guru Gobind Singh's birthday.

FEBRUARY **Hola Mohalla:** the fair in Anandpur in honour of Guru Gobind Singh.

APRIL **Baisakhi:** a celebration of the foundation of the Khalsa.

AUGUST A celebration of the completion of the *Guru Granth Sahib*.

OCTOBER Guru Nanak's birthday.
Diwali: a Hindu festival used by Sikhs to mark the release from prison of Guru Hargobind.

BUDDHISM: AN INTRODUCTION

Buddhism began in northeast India around 450BCE. It is based on the teachings of Siddhartha Gautama, who became known as the Buddha, or 'Enlightened One'. Buddhism emerged from the other religious ideas of the time, predominantly those of the Brahmins. The Buddha frequently overturned or reinterpreted the teachings of others, and his own approach was in many respects quite new. Life, he said, is constantly changing and people should not look for happiness in wealth or possessions, beauty or fame, because these things will disappear. Instead, he taught that we should see things as they really are and, by freeing ourselves from greed, selfishness, ignorance, anger, fear, passion and all the things that keep us attached to this "unreal" world, achieve a state of enlightenment known as *nirvana*.

***Below** This reclining Buddha is from Bangkok in Thailand. The Buddha taught that he was not the only 'Enlightened One'. There were many more buddhas before him and many more to come. The aim of life should be to strive to be an enlightened one, or buddha, oneself.*

After he had achieved enlightenment the Buddha wandered from place to place with a small group of disciples, but during the rainy season settled in one spot where he established a more stable community. This community (*sangha*) became the basis for the monastic life which continues to be important in Buddhism throughout the world today.

The law of cause and effect

Buddhists do not worship a person or a god, but follow a system of thoughts, meditation and spiritual exercise based on the Buddha's teachings, or *dharma*. These teachings were written down long after the Buddha's death. In his lifetime they were passed on by word of mouth by his followers, who carefully memorized them. Buddhism teaches that all our thoughts have consequences both for ourselves and for others. This law of cause and effect, known as *karma*, dictates that the consequence of good deeds, words and thoughts is rebirth into a better life. Similarly, when those who do not accept personal responsibility for the things they do in life are reborn, they will find that they are further away from the ultimate goal of *nirvana*.

Above The monastic life is important in Buddhism. Monks observe a strict way of life that involves having only a few basic possessions and being completely dependent on ordinary people for their one daily meal, shelter and clothing. In return they teach and help the people.

There are five basic rules that all practising Buddhists agree to follow: not to kill; not to steal; not to lie; to abstain from sexual misconduct; and to avoid intoxicants such as drugs and alcohol. The Buddha also taught that compassion and kindness are the most important principles for a person to live by.

Buddhism spread to nearby countries and, eventually, to the West – where it has adapted to the culture of the time and place and become increasingly popular.

Right Buddhism began in India and spread out into the neighbouring countries and beyond. Worldwide there are over 300 million followers. This Buddha on a turquoise throne is from the Chinese Ming Dynasty (1368–1644).

THE LIFE OF THE BUDDHA

There are many myths and legends surrounding the life of the Buddha, but most scholars accept that Buddhism's historical founder lived between 485 and 405 BCE. Siddhartha Gautama came from a prosperous family and led a privileged life. At the age of 29 he is said to have observed three things that prompted him to embark on his spiritual quest: illness; ageing; and death and decay. Tradition has it that he met a holy man who, despite his poverty, was happy. At that moment Siddhartha Gautama realized that life's pleasures are illusions and that the only road to contentment lies in what is real and true. He decided to leave his home and devote himself to the quest for truth.

Left *The Buddha is said to have attained* nirvana *beneath the Bodhi tree, or tree of enlightenment.*

> **"I am is a vain thought. I am not is a vain thought. I shall be is a vain thought. I shall not be is a vain thought. Vain thoughts are a sickness. But after overcoming all vain thoughts one is called a silent thinker."**
>
> The words of the Buddha

The Four Noble Truths

At first he became an ascetic; meditating, fasting and practising severe exercises of self-denial that made his hair fall out and ruined his health, leaving him weak and emaciated. After six years he decided such extremes of self-discipline were unsatisfactory and the best route to enlightenment was along a path of moderation.

One night his life was changed forever when, seated beneath a tree (later called the Bodhi tree, or tree of enlightenment), he began a deep and prolonged meditation. In the course of his meditation he attained a state of perfect knowledge and perfect peace (*nirvana*). This was the moment when he gained insight into The Four Noble Truths – the core of Buddhist teaching.

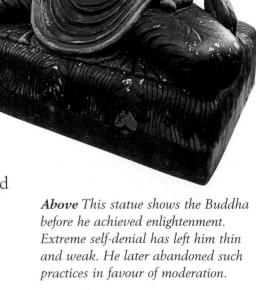

Above *This statue shows the Buddha before he achieved enlightenment. Extreme self-denial has left him thin and weak. He later abandoned such practices in favour of moderation.*

Right The Buddha's teaching is often symbolized by a wheel (seen here in his left hand). In his first sermon in Benares, the Buddha declared that he was setting in motion 'the wheel of dharma'.

THE FOUR NOBLE TRUTHS

• All existence is unsatisfactoriness.
• Unsatisfactoriness is caused by the craving (*tanha*) for something permanent in the world when no such permanence exists.
• The cessation of unsatisfactoriness, *nirvana*, can be attained.
• *Nirvana* can be reached following The Noble Eightfold Path.

THE NOBLE EIGHTFOLD PATH

Each of these eight steps to *nirvana* contains the word *samma*, or right.
Right knowledge
Right attitude
Right speech
Right action
Right livelihood
Right effort
Right state of mind
Right concentration

Shortly after this he gathered round him five companions, who became his first disciples. Travelling round India for the next 45 years, he lived the life of a beggar and teacher. The Buddha died at the age of 80 in the town of Kushinagara. Among his last words to his followers were, "Do not cry. Have I not told you that it is in the nature of all things, however dear they may be to us, that we must part with them and leave them."

THE DEVELOPMENT OF BUDDHISM

After the Buddha's death his followers decided to preserve his teachings. This was not easy because nothing had been written down – indeed it was not until more than 350 years later that the first Buddhist writings appeared. To bring the master's ideas together, Buddhist monks held a council in Rajagriha and agreed that their conclusions should be reviewed 100 years later in Vesali. But it was the third Buddhist council held at Pataliputta that proved the most significant. Monks gathered to try to agree on the Buddha's message, and though at first there was considerable agreement, there were the first signs of a deep division.

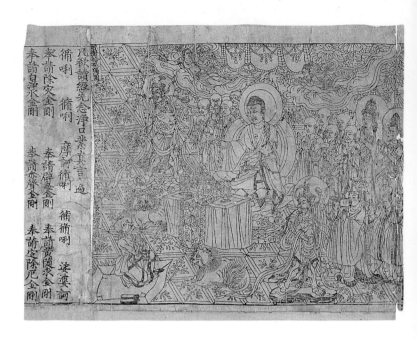

Above A page of the Chinese translation of the so-called Diamond Sutta. *This version appeared in the 9th century* CE *and is the oldest printed book in the world. The* Diamond Sutta *belongs to the collection of Mahayana scriptures known as* The Perfection of Wisdom Suttas.

Two schools of thought

Out of this emerged two distinct forms of Buddhism – early and late. The only surviving school of early Buddhism is known as Theravada, and all later schools are collectively referred to as Mahayana. The main difference between early and late Buddhism is the interpretation of the various teachings. However, they also use different texts. *Theravada* means 'the teaching of the elders'. Its scriptures contain three sets of teachings that were originally written on palm leaves and stored in wicker baskets (hence the other name by which they are known – the *tripitaka*, or three baskets). The *Sutta Pitaka*, or 'basket of doctrinal teachings', is believed to contain the teachings of the Buddha himself. The *Vinaya Pitaka*, or 'basket of monastic disciplinary rules', contains more material about the Buddha and lays down the rules of discipline for the monastic community. The *Abhidhamma Pitaka*, or 'basket of higher teaching', is for serious scholars. The *Mahayana* tradition, or 'Great Vehicle', has its own texts, or *suttas*.

Left The lotus flower, a waterlily with its roots in the mud, features frequently in Buddhist imagery. It symbolizes the belief that enlightenment (the flower) can be achieved in the midst of human suffering (the mud and slime beneath the water).

Above Buddhists believe that stupas (ancient burial mounds) contain relics of early Buddhist holy men, or even of the Buddha himself. Many stupas, like this one in Nepal, have become important places of pilgrimage.

One of the distinctive features of Theravada Buddhism is the idea of the *arhat*. This is a person who has achieved enlightenment through the teaching of another enlightened being (a buddha). Theravadins believe that only monks can achieve such a state and so try to spend some of their life in a monastery. Mahayana Buddhists, on the other hand, believe that everyone is capable of achieving enlightenment. They attach great importance to the concept of the *bodhisattva*, a semi-divine being who has achieved enlightenment but who has voluntarily renounced *nirvana*, to stay in the world to help others. By the 11th century CE, Buddhism had declined in influence in India, but flourished in many other Asian countries.

> "When I attain this highest perfect wisdom, I will deliver all sentient beings into the eternal peace of *nirvana*."
>
> The Buddha's words, taken from the *Diamond Sutta*

TYPES OF BUDDHISM

Buddhism spread beyond India to central and southeast Asia and adapted to the culture of the countries in which it took root. Different varieties of Buddhist practice emerged – the *Mahayana* tradition, in particular, produced several distinctive forms.

Chinese Buddhism

Buddhism arrived in China in the 1st century CE and was practised alongside Confucianism and Taoism (*see* pages 74–81). By the 4th century CE, many of the texts had been translated from Sanskrit into Chinese and many of the *bodhisattvas* had their Chinese equivalents. For example, Avalokiteshvara, the Bodhisattva of Compassion, became Kuan Yin (believed to take the form of a young woman who is ready to help people in trouble).

Tibetan Buddhism

Tibet has its own forms of Buddhism, which combine magic and spirit worship with a type of *Mahayana* Buddhism known as *Vajrayana* ('the vehicle of the thunderbolt'). *Vajrayana* is based on ancient texts called *tantras* and involves ritual practices, such as meditation and chanting *mantras* (words believed to have powerful energies).

Of the many schools of Tibetan Buddhism the best known is the Gelukpa tradition (also known as the Yellow Hats). This monastic tradition stresses the importance of living teachers (*lamas*) to instruct novices in the ways of Buddhist thought. The leader of this school is the Dalai Lama ('lama as great as the ocean'), who is believed to be a reincarnation of the Bodhisattva Avalokiteshvara. When the Dalai Lama dies, other lamas search for a child they believe to be the reincarnation of the 'compassionate one', and he becomes the next Dalai Lama. Following their occupation of Tibet in 1951, the Chinese attempted to control the monasteries, and Tibetan Buddhism is still struggling to keep its traditions intact.

Above *The 14th Dalai Lama, here receiving worshippers, fled from Tibet in 1959 because he and his followers feared persecution by the Chinese.*

Left *The wheel is an important symbol in Buddhism, as it suggests the cycle of birth, death and reincarnation. The 12 spokes may also represent the Four Noble Truths and the Noble Eightfold Path.*

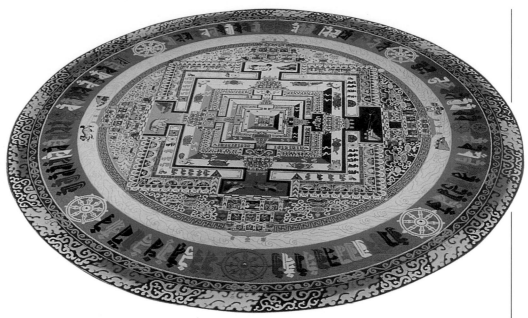

Japanese Buddhism

Buddhism reached Japan in the 6th century CE, arriving from China via Korea. The most popular school of Japanese Buddhism is *Jodo Shu*, or 'Pure Land'. This is based on a *Mahayana* text that tells of a Buddha called Amitabha (or Amida), who lives in a distant world known as the Pure Land. Faith in the Amida Buddha and meditation on his name will, it is believed, lead to rebirth in that heavenly land where *nirvana* can easily be reached. However, the school best known in the West is Zen, which derives its name from the Chinese *ch'an*, meaning 'meditation'. Zen concentrates on meditation and intuition above worship, and prefers study as a way of achieving sudden enlightenment (*satori*). Other means of achieving *nirvana* include *zazen* (sitting cross-legged in the lotus position) and answering a *koan*, or riddle. The purpose of these riddles (such as "What is the sound of one hand clapping?") is to surprise students into looking at things differently, and in doing so to challenge the conventional patterns of thought that prevent them from achieving enlightenment.

Above Mandalas *are maps of the cosmos. They are believed to possess spiritual energy and are used as an aid to meditation in Tantric Buddhism. They are painted, carved, or, as here, made out of sand.*

Left A Zen garden is often used in meditation. Its simple patterns of raked sand suggest the natural shapes of rivers, mountains and waves.*

LIFE IN A BUDDHIST MONASTERY

In some Asian countries, such as Thailand, boys as young as eight are sent to monasteries to learn how to become Buddhist monks. Life for these novice monks is hard. Every morning at five o'clock they are woken by a bell and spend the next two hours until breakfast meditating in silence.

After a breakfast of rice and vegetables, there are prayers, which continue until nine. For the rest of the morning, there are classes where the young monks have to learn Buddhist holy writings word for word. Lunch is followed by an hour-long discussion, during which groups of novices test each other's knowledge of the scriptures and philosophy. In the afternoon there are still more classes, and from five until half-past six, another debate. Dinner is followed by an hour's revision of the sacred texts that they have memorized in the morning. After this the monks may either retire to bed or, if they feel like it, pursue their own meditation in private.

Above *A senior monk teaches two young novices (junior monks) in a monastery in Burma.*

In Tibetan belief, the golden turrets on the roof will lift the building above the waters on the day when a great flood sweeps the land.

Right *The Potala was the centre of Tibetan Buddhism – a tradition with 14 million followers around the world. It was built on a rocky outcrop near Lhasa, the capital of Tibet, and was the traditional home of the Dalai Lama, the spiritual leader of Tibetan Buddhists.*

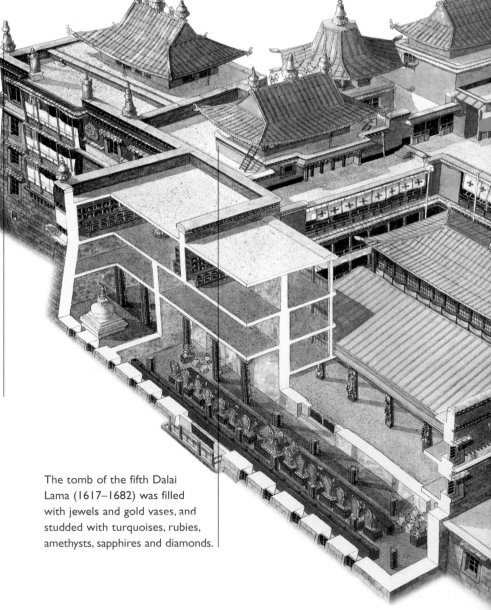

The tomb of the fifth Dalai Lama (1617–1682) was filled with jewels and gold vases, and studded with turquoises, rubies, amethysts, sapphires and diamonds.

Every year, at the start of the rainy season, which usually happens in May, a number of young Burmese boys are ordained as novice monks. After the ceremony – known as *Shin Pyu* – the boys exchange their wreaths of flowers for monks' clothing, and have their heads shaved. Most of these young monks stay in the monastery for only a month or so before returning home. But some remain in the monastery and, at about the age of 20, are fully ordained as adult monks.

The Sangha

The Sangha, as the community of Buddhist monks is called, has formed the backbone of Buddhist society since it was set up by the Buddha himself to preserve and spread his teaching. According to Buddhist doctrine, the life of a monk should be as simple as possible to avoid distraction from spiritual tasks. Life in a Buddhist monastery is not only hard, but also very strict. There are almost 250 rules in the *Vinaya*, the monks' rule book. The monks are not allowed to work for money, to cook their own food or live under the same roof as a woman. One of the most serious offences is quarrelling with someone.

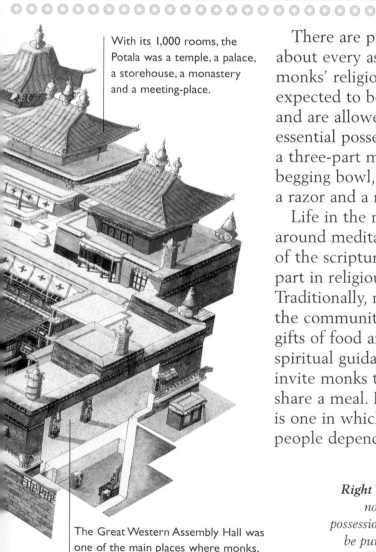

With its 1,000 rooms, the Potala was a temple, a palace, a storehouse, a monastery and a meeting-place.

The Great Western Assembly Hall was one of the main places where monks, officials and pilgrims gathered.

There are precise instructions about every aspect of the monks' religious life. They are expected to beg for their food and are allowed only a few essential possessions, such as a three-part monk's robe, a begging bowl, a water strainer, a razor and a needle.

Life in the monastery revolves around meditation, the study of the scriptures, and taking part in religious ceremonies. Traditionally, monks go out into the community and, in return for gifts of food and clothing, offer spiritual guidance. People may also invite monks to their homes to share a meal. Buddhist society is one in which monks and lay people depend on each other.

Right These young Burmese novices are allowed few possessions because they must be pure in spirit and free of human concerns.

SHINTO: AN INTRODUCTION

Shinto, which means 'way of the gods', originated in prehistoric Japan. According to legend, the gods who controlled the natural elements, such as thunder, wind and rain came down to Earth to inhabit the mountains, streams, rocks, trees and other special parts of the landscape. In time these were given the name *kami* (spirits) and were honoured with their own *jinja* (shrine). Shinto has no founder or divine creator, and no particular set of beliefs, but it is practised by most Japanese people as a folk religion alongside the more formalized rituals of Buddhism. It is quite common for people to turn to Shinto for celebrating births and marriages, and to Buddhism when carrying out funerals.

Shinto legend

Shinto's oldest literary works are the *Kojiki* and the *Nihonshoki*, both written in the 8th century CE. They contain the Japanese creation myths and legends. It is said that Izanagi and his sister Izanami, who were the last of seven generations of the gods, were commanded to form the islands of Japan by dipping a spear into the sea and letting the droplets of saltwater form the land. The supreme deity is believed to be Amaterasu, goddess of the Sun and daughter of Izanagi and Izanami. Amaterasu is honoured at one of Japan's major shrines at Ise, and, even into the 20th century, was said to be a distant ancestor of the ruling imperial family.

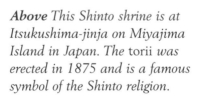

Above This Shinto shrine is at Itsukushima-jinja on Miyajima Island in Japan. The torii *was erected in 1875 and is a famous symbol of the Shinto religion.*

Other lesser spirits are honoured in the hope that they will bring good luck, wealth or happiness. Unless they are approached with great reverence these spirits become very angry. Legend has it that the distinguished poet and teacher Sugawara Michizane, who lived in the 9th century CE, was exiled from court after accusations made by envious courtiers.

Left The most famous mountain in Japan is Mount Fuji. It is also one of the most important natural shrines. Many pilgrims visit the mountain, which has become a symbol of Japan's national identity. This hand-coloured woodblock print, Fuji above the lightning, *is by Hokusai.*

Above This colourful 19th-century print illustrates one of the famous stories from Shinto mythology. The Sun goddess Amaterasu emerges from her cave to bring light and order to the world.

Below This map shows the location of Japanese Shinto shrines that are marked by a torii.

Following Michizane's death, terrible things began to happen to the people of Kyoto. Thunder and lightning struck the palace, storms and droughts affected the city and people began to die in strange circumstances. Only after they had calmed Michizane's angry spirit did the trouble stop. To this day, his shrine is visited by those wishing for success in examinations.

The revival of classical Shinto

In the early centuries of the Common Era, Buddhism, as it spread throughout Japan, absorbed rather than discarded local beliefs. As a result, the *kami* were regarded as buddhas or bodhisattvas and were incorporated into Buddhist practice. By the 19th and 20th centuries, however, scholars had rediscovered the ancient texts and a revival of classical Shinto began. The country looked to its mythical past to build up a strong and proud nation. In 1868, Shinto shrines were cleansed of their Buddhist influences and a system of so-called 'State Shinto' was imposed. Schools taught that the imperial family was related to the gods and insisted on total submission to the will of the emperor, who was believed to be divine. After the defeat of Japan in 1945, the emperor renounced his divine status and an American-style constitution decreed that politics and religion should be separate.

SHINTO WORSHIP

Shinto worship (*matsuri*) is both public and private and revolves around the life-cycle events of a family or community. It is common, for example, for pregnant women to visit a shrine to ask for the safe delivery of their child. Thirty-two days after a male child is born (33 days for a girl), the baby is carried to the shrine by the mother or grandmother for a *hatsu miya-mairi*, or first shrine visit, and brought into the presence of the *kami* for a blessing. Later in childhood, the *shichi-go-san* (seven–five–three) festival is held. Parents with three- or seven-year-old sons, or five-year-old daughters, bring them to the shrine for a purification rite, or *harai*. During this service, a wand with paper streamers may be waved over the children's heads to remove bad influences from their lives and to purify them for the future.

Above Shinto worshippers hang up a prayer board, or ema, *outside a shrine and write their requests on it.*

Below The Tori no Ichi *festival was originally a celebration of the god of battle but now celebrates good luck. Here a man holds a lucky charm made of straw.*

Entering the shrine

Elaborate rituals surround entry to the shrine. It is approached through a *torii*, a wooden or stone archway that separates the outside world from the sacred space within. At the entrance is a trough of running water where worshippers wash their hands and rinse their mouths. Then they proceed to the prayer hall, or *haiden*, where the *kami* is alerted to their presence by two claps of the hands. After putting money into the offertory box, ringing a bell and making a deep ritual bow to the *kami*, worshippers can offer up their prayers. In one part of the shrine complex is a wall on which visitors can hang an *ema*. This is a five-sided wooden board on which worshippers write their requests, which may be anything from curing a disease or giving up smoking, to winning the lottery. At the New Year festival these prayer boards are burned to make room for the following year's prayers.

Above This shrine has a shimenawa – *a thick rope threaded with folded white paper to denote a sacred space.*

The *honden*

Beyond the *haiden* is the *honden*, the main hall where the *kami* lives. Only priests may enter this space. During festival times, the image of the *kami* is taken out of the main shrine and placed in a *mikoshi*, or portable shrine. It is then paraded through the town so that the whole community can be blessed by the spirit. *Fudas*, or charms, are on sale to help bring good luck or ward off evil spirits. These are then taken home and put on a *kami* shelf, where they remain for a year, protecting the family from misfortune.

Sometimes, when it is not possible to come to a shrine, a priest goes out to offer prayers in the name of the *kami*. He might go to a construction site to purify it and to ask for the building (a bank, say, or the headquarters of an industrial corporation) to be blessed by the spirit's presence. Priests will even bless a new car in the hope that it will not be involved in an accident.

Above A priest burns last year's prayer boards in a ceremony at the Shinto shrine in Ise, Japan.

Right Children's Day takes place once a year in November at the Meiji shrine, the most popular shrine in Tokyo. Parents bring their children to receive a blessing for the future.

71

CHINESE RELIGIONS: AN INTRODUCTION

Chinese religion is not one single system of belief, like Judaism, Christianity or Islam. It contains four main elements that are practised alongside each other. These are Confucianism, Taoism, Buddhism and folk religion. Chinese people have been influenced by the ideas contained in all four traditions and often combine the rituals of one with the ceremonies of another.

Early history

Until the late 19th century China was ruled by powerful clans or families, known as dynasties. The earliest record of religious activity dates from the Shang Dynasty around the second millennium BCE. The discovery of oracle bones and shells provides evidence that the ancient Chinese practised a system of divination, or forecasting the future, and believed that unseen spirits affected the lives of ordinary people. Before someone embarked on a new project or set out on a journey, a diviner (someone skilled in the interpretation of supernatural messages) asked the spirits what was in store for them. A bone or turtle shell was heated until it cracked, then the diviner looked at the pattern of the cracks and interpreted the spirit's answer. The question and answer were engraved on the bone or shell and were then stored away. The spirits were apparently consulted on all aspects of human life, including warfare, medicine, farming and even the weather.

Above Firecrackers are lit to celebrate the New Year festival in honour of the kitchen god, Tsao Chun. He watches what goes on in the household and is believed to control people's lives. At New Year he is thought to report back to heaven, which will grant good fortune for good behaviour and bad luck for bad deeds.

Left Ancestor worship is important in Chinese religion, and people regularly pay their respects at the graveside. Families also have shrines in their homes to honour their dead parents.

The importance of ancestors

As well as forecasting the future, the Chinese looked to their past. Confucius (551–479BCE), from whom the belief system known as Confucianism takes its name, encouraged the practice of ancestor worship that had been in existence since ancient times. Confucius was a sage, or wise man, who taught that kindness (*jen*) towards humanity is one of the most important qualities to develop. He also taught the principle of filial piety, or respect for parents. If children honoured their father and mother, he believed, they would become respectful adults who would, in turn, respect their legitimate rulers and form the basis of a stable society. This respect for parents and elders carried on even after death in the form of ancestor worship. To this day, elaborate rituals surround Chinese funerals and many people believe that if a body is buried without proper ceremony it will not find its way to Heaven, but will hang around as a troublesome ghost.

Three different religions

Taoism is said to have been founded by Lao-tzu in the 6th century BCE. The Tao means 'the way', and reaching it through meditation, chanting and physical exercise is thought to be a means of achieving immortality. Buddhism came to China in the 1st century CE and influenced the development of both Confucianism and Taoism. The fourth tradition – popular or folk religion – involves worshipping a variety of gods drawn from myths and legends.

Above Confucius, Lao-tzu and the Buddha all lived at around the same time. This symbolic picture shows how different religions have co-existed in China.

Right Oracle bones were used by the ancient Chinese as a way of divining the future.

THE DEVELOPMENT OF CONFUCIANISM

The Western name given to this Chinese tradition of belief emerged in the 16th and 17th centuries CE, when Christian missionaries began to come across the writings of K'ung Fu-tzu whose name they translated into Latin. Confucius was not a prophet or a messiah, but a mild-mannered teacher who believed that kindness (*jen*) towards one's fellow human beings and respect for parents (filial piety) were the basis of a harmonious society. He was born into a minor aristocratic family and spent his early life as a civil servant in government offices. It was not until he reached the age of 50, that Confucius became well known and travelled the country spreading his ideas.

Above *This illustration shows Emperor Teaon-Kwang reviewing his guards at the Palace of Peking. The Confucian model of the ideal state centred on a just emperor ruling his people wisely and with compassion. A harmonious rule would be granted by 'the Heavenly Mandate', or divine approval. If the Heavenly Mandate were withdrawn disaster might occur.*

Heaven and Earth

Confucianism is primarily concerned with moral conduct on Earth, but it also contains a spiritual dimension in that Confucius believed that humanity was guided by a higher power that he called 'Heaven'. This early teaching was developed by another teacher called Meng-tzu (c.371–289BCE), later known in the West as Mencius, who believed there was a direct connection between that divine power and human life.

The early Confucians taught that Heaven disapproved of chaos and approved of harmony. Harmony came to be seen as a balance of two opposite but complementary forces known as the yin and the yang.

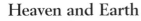

Left *Confucius, portrayed here in a 17th-century scroll, put great emphasis on harmony in the family and in society.*

Above *The unity of opposite but complementary forces – the yin and the yang – is represented in this symbol. Each half contains the 'seed' of its opposite.*

Reading the signs

It was believed that divine approval of a government was signalled by the 'Heavenly Mandate', which rewarded an emperor with good weather, generous harvests, obedient subjects and so on. Teams of government officials trained in Confucian thought travelled the country looking for signs or portents. After monitoring the mood of the people, the state of the crops and even the weather, they could then report back to the emperor, who then had an indication as to how his rule was

Above *This 17th-century painting shows different generations (sage, scholar and infant) studying the yin and yang symbol. In traditional Chinese thought, yang represents all that is above, hot, light, hard, active and male. Yin stands for all that is below, cold, dark, soft, passive and female. Opposites were considered to be complementary aspects of a single whole.*

progressing. In time, this monitoring process was more formally established as a system known as 'The Theory of Portents'.

Confucian philosophy was consolidated from the 11th century CE onwards, with teachers such as Chu Hsi (1130–1200) and Wang Yang-ming (1472–1529). These teachers (collectively known as the Neo-, or new, Confucians) combined early Confucian thought with elements of Taoism and Buddhism and produced a system that lasted from the medieval period to the late 19th century.

CONFUCIAN PRACTICE

The essential message of Confucianism is that all things visible (on Earth) and invisible (in Heaven) are interdependent. In the sphere of personal behaviour, it teaches that right conduct on Earth – which involves respect and compassion – is its own reward and is in keeping with the ultimate harmony of the Universe. In the sphere of public affairs, Confucianism says that a just emperor will be blessed with a stable and strong empire – according to the terms of the Heavenly Mandate.

The texts

The practice of divination was an important way for individuals and governments to read the mind of the heavenly forces. The methods are explained in one of the five Confucian scriptures: the *I Ching* or *Book of Changes*. The others are the *Shih Ching* (*Book of Odes*), the *Shu Ching* (*Book of History*), the *Li Chi* (*Book of Rites*) and the *Ch'un-ch'iu* (*The Annals of Spring and Autumn*). These classic texts, together with the *Four Books of Confucianism*, are the backbone of Confucian literature. They contain poetry, philosophy, rules for divination and ritual, history and the sayings of Confucius and his followers, as well as stories about the origins of Chinese society.

Above *Education is central to Confucianism. Pupils are encouraged to study hard and to show respect to their teachers and elders.*

Left *The practice of divination (foretelling the future), which was put into systematic form in the* I Ching, *continues in popular form today. Fortune-tellers and geomancers (those advising on where to site objects and houses to bring good fortune) are common features of Chinese life.*

Above *The man on the right is about to throw down the sticks he is holding. The pattern of sticks will be matched against the predictions in the* I Ching *(Book of Changes) to determine what the future holds. The* I Ching *is an elaborate system of divination (foretelling the future) that uses sticks or coins to produce combinations of straight (yang) lines or broken (yin) lines. Consulting the* I Ching *was an important part of state practice.*

Good behaviour

Just as the relationship between Heaven and Earth was important so, too, were relationships between human beings. Confucius' golden rule is contained in his words, "Do not do to others what you do not wish to be done to you." This basic moral principle runs through all Confucian scripture.

Confucianism is characterized by its great respect for learning and study. Under the emperors, up until the late 19th century CE, an elaborate examination system was the basis of employment and promotion. The authorities encouraged the study of Confucian texts and tested potential recruits on aspects of Confucian philosophy. Although criticized by some for its inflexibility, the examination system succeeded in promoting an ethic of hard work and public service so that, even after the Communist takeover of China, the principles of hard work and study still survived.

THE ORIGINS OF TAOISM

Tao means 'the Way', in which people live a life of moderation, avoiding extremes of any kind. The secret of happiness is to live naturally without trying to be different or change things. Although very little is known about his life, the founder of Taoism is traditionally taken to be the poet and sage Lao-tzu, to whom is attributed the central text of Taoism, the *Tao-te-Ching* (Classic of the Way and its Power), dating from around the 6th century BCE.

Above Mountains and rivers hold a special spiritual significance in Taoism. Sages sought comfort in the magnificence of the natural world and, freed from the tyranny of acquiring material possessions, could reflect on the harmony of Heaven, nature and humankind.

Philosophy or religion

There are two elements to Tao. The first, *Tao-chia* or philosophical Taoism, develops the political idea of a sage ruler or emperor ruling through wisdom, not force. The second, *Tao-chiao*, promotes a more mystical or religious understanding of the world. With proper practice, it says, people can free themselves from the dreary acquisition of material possessions and find liberation on a spiritual level, culminating in immortality.

The texts

The *Tao-Te-Ching* and the *Chuang Tzu*, the two classic Taoist texts, teach that by harmonizing the forces of yin and yang (*see* page 74) a person can achieve a state of mind that takes good fortune and bad in its stride without complaint. Long life and immortality are believed to be the rewards of following the Tao. Immortality is understood in two ways: eternal life in a transformed body; and, in a more symbolic sense, release from the worries of the everyday world, and spiritual liberation that exists outside time.

Left Ge Changgeng was a calligrapher and wise man who wrote works on Taoism. He associated with Liu Hai, one of the Immortals, whose symbol was the three-legged toad, a mystical creature thought to exist only on the Moon. The toad is also the symbol of money-making and is shown here with a string of gold coins on its head.

> "To be unsnared by vulgar ways, to make no vain show of material things, to bring no hardship on others … There were those who believed that the 'art of the Way' lay in those things."
>
> *Chuang Tzu*

Doing and being

Taoists teach that to achieve progress one should practise *wu-wei*, or 'active inaction'. This seems contradictory, but it involves making a positive attempt not to fight against the flow of universal energy (*ch'i*), but move with it and enter into a balanced state of being. This is illustrated in the writings of Chuang-tzu, who describes the work of a palace cook, a master butcher named Ting. Ting is so skilful in the art of carving that his knife seems to encounter no resistance as it slices up an ox for the evening's banquet. The king is amazed and asks the cook where he learned such skills. Ting replies that by concentrating on the right way (the Tao) of doing the job he can effortlessly find the empty spaces between the muscle and the flesh. He does not have to think with his active mind about the business of carving, rather he allows his spirit or consciousness (*shen*) to take him along, with the result that the beast is effortlessly sliced. In other words, he is *being* a butcher rather than *doing* the butchering. Taoism teaches people to go beyond mere intellect and to appeal to a higher power or consciousness that will take them along with the flow of life.

Right Little is known about Lao-tzu, the founder of Taoism, but one of the legends portrays him as a scholar in the Chou Dynasty. Travelling on an ox, he is said to have come to a border post where he was asked to write down his teaching. This he did in the form of the Tao-te-Ching. After that he vanished and was never seen again.

79

TAOIST PRACTICE

Taoists believe that an energy (*ch'i*) runs through the whole of creation. It is found in mountains and plains, in rivers and streams, in trees and flowers, in Heaven and Earth, and, crucially, in human beings. Harnessing this vital energy harmoniously (with the appropriate balance of yin and yang) is the key to a long and ultimately happy life.

Harmony and balance
To achieve harmony, certain Taoist groups have developed elaborate rituals involving meditation, chanting, physical exercise and natural medicine. The mere chanting of certain Taoist texts is believed to bring about a physical and mental change in a person, promoting the harmony of yin and yang that is the goal of religious Taoism. When these forces are not in harmony things start to go wrong. An imbalance of yin and yang, for example, is believed to be at the root of some diseases that will be cured when the balance is restored. Destructive energy, often in the form of an unquiet spirit, is thought to be a result of an excess of yin.

Above It is common to see groups of people of all ages practising t'ai ch'i in public places. This stylized series of exercises was originally a martial art and is practised to harmonize the yin and yang forces in the human body, as well as to promote health and long life.

Left Taoist priests play an important role in Chinese communal worship. Their function is to perform the harmonizing rites that will ensure health and long life for the community.

Achieving immortality

Whereas Confucians strive to become sages or wise people at the service of society, the Taoist strives to become an immortal (a *hsien*). Confucianism places greater emphasis on the organization of the ideal state than Taoism, which is more concerned with the individual and their personal development. Some Taoists interpret the notion of immortality literally and go to great lengths to achieve it. In the past, stories circulated of secret rituals known only to a select group of devotees who drank herbal potions to become immortal. There were tales of supernatural feats of levitation where their bodies would rise up into the air by magic. Some of these Taoist societies still exist today.

Natural medicine

Most practising Taoists do not go to such extremes. They believe the body is like the natural landscape, criss-crossed by invisible channels of vital energy that control bodily functions. At certain points along these channels, rather like sluice gates along a canal, are points where the flow of energy can be interrupted and controlled in order to re-establish the correct combination of yin and yang. At these points, acupuncturists (traditional healers) insert fine needles to treat various ailments. Taoism says that nothing is fixed. Life is in constant flux and humanity should go with its flow.

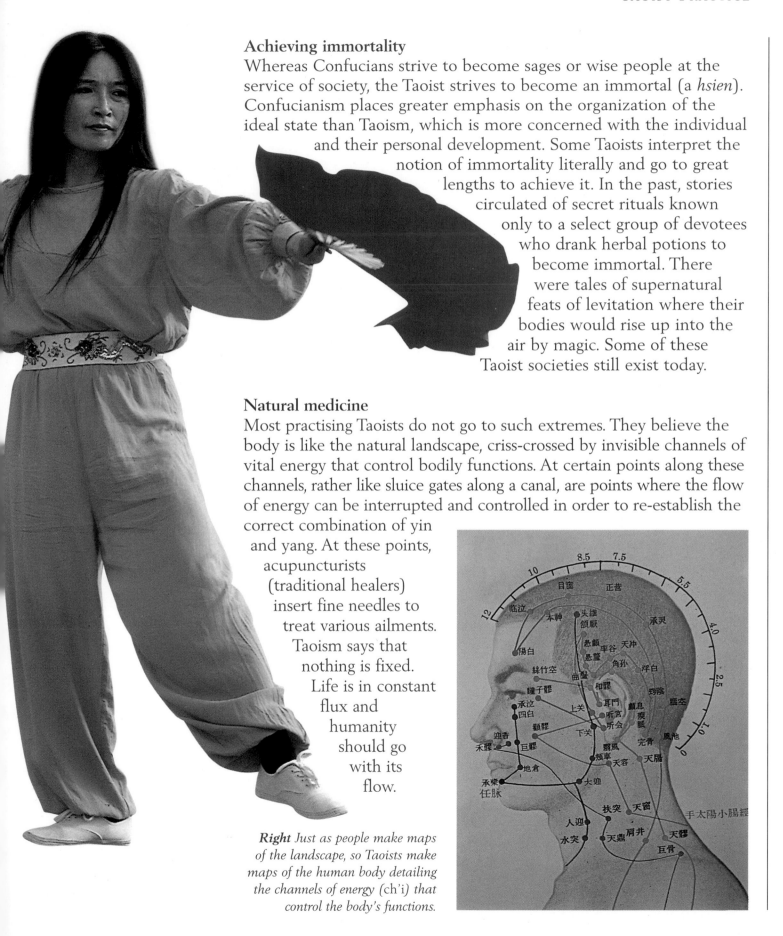

Right *Just as people make maps of the landscape, so Taoists make maps of the human body detailing the channels of energy (ch'i) that control the body's functions.*

REFORM AND REVOLUTION

The main religions in China have always influenced each other and people often practise a form of religion that contains elements of each. The religions themselves have also developed or altered over the centuries, producing schools of thought that some have followed and some rejected. For example, the Confucianism of Confucius and Mencius was reformed again in the 12th and 15th centuries CE by two Neo-Confucians – Chu Hsi and Wang Yang-ming (*see* page 75). Both agreed that wisdom and compassion were the main goals of life, but they disagreed on how best to achieve them. Chu Hsi founded the *li-hsueh* school of teaching which argued that, to practise benevolence (*jen*) towards humanity, people had to go through a long process of self-development. Only after many years of refining one's understanding of the world, he believed, could one's own human nature be refined to the point where true benevolence and compassion were possible. The school of Wang Yang-ming – the *hsin hsueh* – disagreed with this gradual approach and taught that sudden enlightenment was possible if the mind was brought into harmony with the Tao. This fusion of Confucian and Taoist principle is typical of the direction Chinese religion has taken.

Above China's Communist Party disapproved of religion, but its leader from 1949, Mao Tse-tung, was venerated in a way that was almost religious. Here his portrait hangs above a family shrine.

A single framework
In the 16th century, philosopher Lin Chao-en tried to bring Confucianism, Buddhism and Taoism into a single framework. He combined the meditation and self-development practised by Buddhist monks and Taoist masters with the selflessness and public service of the Confucians. Even today many people borrow freely from each tradition.

Right During the seven-week festival of Da beiba, Taoist priests bless offerings made to the gods and pray for peace.

Religion under threat

The upheavals of the 20th century have had a great effect on the religious lives of ordinary people in China. Mao Tse-tung's Communist Party, which came to power in 1949, disapproved of religion. Communists have described religion as 'the opium of the people' – a powerful but dangerous drug that prevents people from seeing the world as it really is and stops them from launching a revolutionary challenge to the forces of injustice in the world.

The Cultural Revolution of 1966 tried to rid the country of what it believed to be backward and conservative religious practices. Temples were destroyed, Confucius was denounced, believers were persecuted and life for the faithful was made extremely difficult. Ironically, the cult of Chairman Mao had some of the marks of a religious movement. He was venerated in schools, factories and farms, and his image, which appeared on signs and billboards in villages, towns and cities, had the look of a religious icon portraying a saviour of the people.

But religious belief is remarkably resilient and the authorities were eventually forced to accept it as a fact of life. Religious groups had to be registered with the state. In effect this meant that religious believers could practise their faith in return for a degree of state control. The Chinese authorities have been very wary of foreign influence, and the Vatican in Rome had been allowed little formal control of Catholicism within China. Those Chinese people choosing to worship outside the supervision of the state formed underground groups that functioned in secret. Their members risked severe penalties if their activities were discovered, but many persisted, believing that religious freedom is a basic human right which should not be suppressed.

Below Colourful masks are worn to represent different gods in a long procession through the streets of Taipei in Taiwan. One of the largest religious events of the year, the festival celebrates the birthday of the god, Chingshan Wang, and is held on the 22nd day of the 10th lunar month (usually November or December).

83

POPULAR RELIGIONS IN CHINA

Chinese popular or folk religion is not found in any specific religious text. Over the years it has grown out of a mixture of superstition and established religious practices of the day.

Elemental worship

In ancient China people lived close to nature and believed that heavenly spirits controlled the wind and the rain. They depended on the land for their livelihood. Extremes of heat, cold, or rain could destroy crops and threaten their survival. In times of need they asked the heavenly spirits for help, and in times of plenty they gave them thanks. Local cults grew up that looked to a particular spirit (sometimes the spirit of a dead ancestor, who could intervene in Heaven) to ensure that crops would be healthy and harvests bountiful.

Domestic gods

Believers might have a shrine to a particular god whom they would approach in a ritual way, bowing respectfully before asking for a favour and leaving an offering of food or flowers. The gods of happiness (Fu Hsing), of wealth (Tsai Shen) and of long life (Shou Hsing) are popular figures in Chinese folk religion and are often worshipped at family birthdays and the New Year. As well as appealing to the gods for help and good fortune, people also look to them for protection against evil spirits.

Left A festival lion is paraded through the streets of Hong Kong to mark the New Year. Houses and shops are decorated with vegetables and red money packets and, when the lion dances by and takes these, it brings good luck.

Above At this funeral, paper 'money' is being ritually burned as an offering to the gods of the underworld.

Below The god of wealth, Tsai Chen, is a popular figure in Chinese folk religion and often represented at festivals.

Helping the spirits

Funeral rites are treated with special attention because any failure to send a person to the heavenly realm in the proper way may result in that person's unquiet spirit remaining on Earth to bring misfortune to the family. Before the soul of the deceased arrives safely in Heaven it must first descend to the underworld, where it has to explain its actions in life. Those who have maintained good behaviour during their lifetime are guaranteed a faster journey to Heaven. It is believed that the soul of the dead person can be helped along its way by the living, who will offer up paper 'money' to the gods of the underworld to bribe them into letting their dead relatives through. They may also build paper models of cars or planes to ensure transport to Heaven.

Spiritual powers

In popular religion, the gods (*shen*) symbolize order in the face of the chaos that is caused by evil spirits. Some of these popular gods are believed to cure common illnesses, and others, such as Tsou-chen, to control epidemics of smallpox.

Also popular is the practice of *feng shui* (wind and water). *Feng shui* involves the positioning of buildings or objects in the home or in other places such as the office, in a particular way that will be in harmony with the Earth's natural forces (*ch'i*). If sitings are correct, this is said to balance the yin and the yang in nature and bring the person involved good fortune.

Above The smiling Chinese god of long life holds a staff and a peach from which a crane chick is hatching.

JUDAISM: AN INTRODUCTION

Judaism is the world's oldest monotheistic religion – that is to say, it is the first of the world's great faiths to accept as its central belief that there is only one god who created the world and who continues to rule over it. Judaism began with Abraham, who can properly be called the first Jew. God promised Abraham that, in return for his obedience, He would make him the father (patriarch) of a great nation. He commanded Abraham to leave his home (Ur of the Chaldees in modern-day Iraq between the Tigris and Euphrates rivers) and to travel to a land He had promised to him – Israel. Abraham agreed, thus accepting the Covenant (agreement) that God had made with him and, by extension, with the people of Israel. As a sign of the Covenant, every male Jew has to be circumcized.

Since, out of all the families, tribes and nations who could have been offered the Covenant, Abraham alone was chosen for the honour (and also the responsibility), his descendants, the Jews, consider themselves to be the 'Chosen People'.

Above This boy is carrying the Torah Scrolls to a service, where they will focus the hearts and minds of the congregation on the word of God. On their thirteenth birthdays, boys are allowed to read from the Torah Scrolls for the first time.

Revelation on Mount Sinai

According to the Hebrew Bible, the word of God was revealed to Moses on Mount Sinai some 3,500 years ago. It is said that at that moment God handed over not only the Ten Commandments but also the first five books of scripture, known as the Torah.

From tribe to nation

The 'Israelites' began as a small family, undergoing captivity in Egypt and wandering in the desert before they arrived in the Promised Land of Canaan, where King Saul, and then King David, built them into a nation.

Left This Jewish Ethiopian boy is holding the scrolls. The Jews are not a race. They are best described as a people or a family from many different races and lands united by a shared sense of belief and tradition.

Around 950BCE, David's son, Solomon, built a magnificent Temple. This was destroyed in 586BCE by the Babylonians, who took the Jews into captivity. A second Temple was built but this was destroyed by the Romans in 70CE, leading to another great dispersal (*diaspora*) of the Jews throughout the Middle East and Europe.

Unity in adversity

Despite the fact that the Jews were spread far and wide, they tried (not always successfully) to stay true to God's law. Eventually, the interpretation of the law contained in the Torah was debated and written down by the rabbis (teachers) and gathered together into a collection of writings known as the Talmud. Study of the Talmud gave a unity to Jewish practice.

Death and regeneration

The biggest challenge to the Jewish people in the modern age came in the late 1930s, when the Nazis under Adolf Hitler began what they hoped would be the complete extermination of the Jews. More than six million Jews were murdered in what has come to be called the Holocaust. And yet, although comparatively few in number (today there are only some 12 million worldwide), the Jews have exerted a spiritual, ethical and intellectual influence out of all proportion to their numbers. Their religious practices have been adapted to suit modern times, but the core of the Jewish faith recalls a pivotal event in human history – when a people submitted themselves to the word of God and were inspired to lead their lives by it.

Right The Star of David was first used as a symbol of Jewish identity in the 14th century. Originally it was used as a magical sign in the Middle East, where it was known as Solomon's Seal.

THE HISTORY OF JUDAISM

Judaism began with Abraham, who was uneasy with the many pagan gods of his homeland in Mesopotamia and responded to the call of the one true god to leave home and follow him. The story of his departure is contained in the Book of Genesis where God says, "Leave your country, your people and your father's household, and go to the land I will show you." (Genesis 12:1). Abraham's grandson Jacob (subsequently named Israel by God) had twelve sons whose families became the twelve tribes of Israel. Several generations later the twelve tribes were taken into slavery by the Egyptians. Eventually, they were led out of Egypt (the Exodus) by Moses, who later received God's Ten Commandments on Mount Sinai. After 40 long years of wandering in the desert, the Israelites entered the 'Promised Land' of Canaan – not led by Moses, who did not live to take them there, but by Joshua. Gradually, the Israelites grew in strength as God had promised and, after rule by leaders known as Judges, looked for a king to govern them.

A nation divided

The Israelites hoped that this king, ritually blessed and anointed, would triumph over their enemies and establish God's kingdom of divine justice. The succession of kings anointed in this way (beginning with Saul) symbolized the Jewish expectation that God's righteousness would eventually be a reality on Earth. David was the first of the great kings and made Jerusalem his capital. His son Solomon built the first Temple there. When Solomon died (c.930BCE), the nation was split into two by an internal rebellion. Jeroboam and ten of the twelve tribes established the Kingdom of Israel in the north, while the descendants of Rehoboam founded Judah in the south.

Above The great rebellion against the Romans ended at Masada, a desert fortress by the Dead Sea. Rather than surrender, the entire camp committed suicide. Masada has since become a symbol of heroism and resistance.

Left The menorah (a candlestick with seven branches) was first used in the Tabernacle in the desert and later installed in Solomon's Temple, Jerusalem.

There was great tension between the prophets and the kings. The prophets criticized their rulers for worshipping false idols and for straying from the path of God. The Kingdom of Judah (from which Judaism takes its name) outlived that of Israel, whose ten tribes vanished from history. But Judah was itself overrun by the Babylonians, who captured the Jews and destroyed the Temple in 586BCE.

Above *According to scripture, David killed the giant Goliath, a warrior of the Philistines, with a single sling shot. David eventually became king of the Israelites and made Jerusalem his capital city.*

Exile and return

Fifty years later, the Babylonians were themselves captured by the Persians, who gave permission for the Jews to return home. Some Jews did so and they began to rebuild the Temple. Others stayed in Babylon until around 458BCE when, under Ezra and Nehemiah, they returned and put the law of the Torah and worship of God at the centre of their religious and political lives.

In the next centuries further invasions took place, threatening to destroy Jewish identity with Greek philosophy and alien forms of worship. In 165BCE, Judas Maccabaeus led a revolt against the Syrians and restored the Temple to its original purity. This victory is remembered each year at the festival of Chanukah (*see* page 103).

Below *Moses, a towering figure in Jewish history, leads his people out of slavery in Egypt. Behind the Israelites, Pharaoh's army drowns in the Red Sea.*

Dispersal

The country came under Roman control in 63BCE. Roman rule was hard to accept and the Jews mounted a series of rebellions that ended in 135CE. In 70CE, the Romans had destroyed Jerusalem and its temple and killed many of the inhabitants. Other Jews dispersed throughout the Middle East and Europe, and developed their own religious life and hoped that one day they would return to their homeland. The state of Israel was finally founded in 1948.

THE DIASPORA

The destruction of the Temple by the Romans in 70CE was a decisive event in the history of Judaism. At a stroke, Jews lost the unifying feature of their spiritual life – Temple worship – and were also in danger of losing their identity.

The rabbinic tradition

A decision by Johanan ben Zakkai to set up a religious academy on the Judean coast in Yavneh, however, provided a solution. The academy, staffed by rabbis or teachers, soon became a focus of learning and shared tradition within the Jewish world. Although it declined in importance after the failure of the last Jewish revolt against the Romans in 135CE, other academies in Galilee took its place and a sense of continuity was maintained.

The Golden Age

When the Roman Emperor Constantine converted to Christianity in 313CE, making it the state religion a decade later, life became hard for the Jews. By now, many had already dispersed, settling around the Mediterranean, particularly in Spain. Persecution became commonplace and they were not to know real stability until the middle of the 7th century CE when the Muslim Arab invasions transformed the map of Europe. The Jews flourished under the Moors to such an extent that the 10th and 11th centuries were known as Spain's 'Golden Age', when philosophers and religious leaders from both Islam and Judaism shared each others' ideas and lived together in harmony.

Above This 14th-century illumination shows a service in a synagogue in northern Spain. Jews and Muslims lived together in harmony, and the influence of Islamic or Moorish art on the synagogue is clear.

Left The destruction of the Temple in 70CE is depicted on the victory arch of Titus in Rome. Roman soldiers carry off the Temple menorah.

MAIMONIDES' 13 PRINCIPLES OF FAITH

1. God exists.
2. He is one.
3. He is unique and incorporeal (i.e. not made out of flesh and blood like humans).
4. He is eternal.
5. He alone should be worshipped.
6. The prophets spoke God's revealed word.
7. Moses was the greatest of the prophets.
8. God revealed Himself to Moses and gave him the Torah.
9. Neither God nor the Torah will change.
10. God knows everything.
11. People will be rewarded for good deeds and punished for bad.
12. The Messiah will come to Earth.
13. The dead will be resurrected.

Below Jews are herded from the Warsaw Ghetto in 1943 by German SS soldiers. It is estimated that 1.2 million Jews were murdered in the Holocaust.

Sephardi and Ashkenazi

The *diaspora* (dispersal) of the Jews outside Israel produced two distinct traditions: the Sephardi Jews of Spain and the Mediterranean who spoke in a mixture of old Spanish and Hebrew known as Ladino, and the Ashkenazi Jews who settled in central Europe and Germany and spoke in a mixture of German and Hebrew dialect known as Yiddish.

Philosophy and mysticism

Spain's Golden Age did not last but it provided a period of stability that produced many outstanding Jewish scholars. One of these was Moses Maimonides (1135–1204), who is famous for the *Guide for the Perplexed*, a book that tries to show that the ancient Torah is compatible with modern philosophy. Maimonides also drew up the 13 principles of the faith, which are the cornerstone of Jewish belief even today.

Spain also produced the mystical tradition known as the Kabbalah, which tries to go beyond mere intellect in search of a personal, spiritual union with God. The main Kabbalist text is the *Zohar* (Book of Divine Splendour), finished by Rabbi Moses de Leon of Granada (1250–1305). It sees God as *Eyn Sof*, or The Infinite One, and attributes to God specific characteristics (the ten *Sefirot* or 'emanations'): the supreme crown of the divine name; wisdom; intelligence; love; power; beauty; endurance; majesty; foundation and kingdom.

Dispersal again

The Christian conquest of Muslim Spain ended in 1492 when the Jews were forced to convert to Christianity or leave the country. Another dispersal followed, taking the Jews all round the Mediterranean and beyond. For the best part of two centuries Jewish communities attempted to reconstruct and maintain themselves, while keeping alive the hope that the Messiah would free them from their enemies and create a better world.

THE TORAH

The Torah is the name given to the first five books of the Hebrew Bible – Genesis, Exodus, Leviticus, Numbers and Deuteronomy. They are believed by strict Jews to be the word of God as revealed to Moses on Mount Sinai. Progressive or liberal Jews believe that the word of God was not revealed at one particular time, but is part of a continuing process which successive generations work out under God's inspiration.

The Ten Commandments

As well as creation stories, Jewish history, poetry and family sagas, the first five books also contain the Ten Commandments. These lay down the basic rules that people and societies must follow for their own good. More than this, they set down religious and moral codes that Jews should follow if they wish to do God's will.

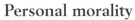

Personal morality

The Ten Commandments have a central place in the Torah, but there are also many other rules within the five books that are important. These are the basis of 613 *mitzvot* (rules) covering areas of personal morality, such as loving your neighbour as yourself, or treating people with kindness and respect. The *mitzvot* govern relationships between husband and wife, and parents and children. They state what rituals Jews should carry out, what they should wear, how they should worship, how animals should be slaughtered and what foods can and cannot be eaten.

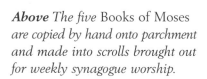

***Above** The five Books of Moses are copied by hand onto parchment and made into scrolls brought out for weekly synagogue worship.*

***Right** Studying the Torah is the work of a lifetime.*

Left *Left The study of the Torah is central to Jewish faith. Students are encouraged to read and re-read it in order to understand how God's law can be put into practice in everyday life.*

The 'Oral Torah'

As well as the five books known as the 'Written Torah', Moses is also thought by Orthodox Jews to have received from God the 'Oral Torah'. This is an interpretation of the laws which have been passed on by teachers down the generations. It is believed that the Torah contains all the guidelines Jews need to deal with every aspect of human life.

> **"I am the Lord your God ... You shall have no other gods before me."**
>
> God to Moses on Mount Sinai, Exodus 20.2-3

It instructs Jews how they are to live a life pleasing to God, as an example to the world.

As a reminder of how sacred it is to the Jewish people, a copy of the Torah is kept in a container called an ark in every synagogue. Rabbis argue over the exact meaning of the text. Orthodox Jews believe that the Torah, being divinely inspired, is as valid today as it was in the ancient world. Those who take a more liberal view say that some of the strict rules have to be adapted for Jews to come to terms with the modern world.

Left Moses is traditionally said to have received the Ten Commandments directly from God on Mount Sinai. These established a framework of law on which a civilized society could be built.

THE TEN COMMANDMENTS
Exodus Chapter 20, verses 2–17

1. I am the Lord your God. You shall have no other gods before me.
2. You shall not make a graven image.
3. You shall not take the name of the Lord your God in vain.
4. Keep the Sabbath Day holy. Do not work on the Sabbath.
5. Honour your father and mother.
6. You shall not kill.
7. You shall not commit adultery.
8. You shall not steal.
9. You shall not bear false witness.
10. You shall not covet your neighbour's property.

PATRIARCHS, PROPHETS AND KINGS

Throughout the 4,000 years of its history, Judaism has produced a number of powerful individuals who have made their mark on the faith and shaped it into what it is today.

Abraham, Isaac and Jacob

The first of the patriarchs was Abraham, who some time around 2000BCE left the city of Ur of the Chaldees to go where God had chosen to send him. His story is told in the Book of Genesis, which is partly an early tribal history of the people of Israel. Abraham was 75 years old, and although he and his wife Sarah had no children he was told that he would be the father of a great nation. When Abraham was 100 years old, he and Sarah had their first child Isaac, who was very precious to Abraham because he would be the next in line to carry out God's plan. According to the Hebrew Bible, Abraham was commanded to sacrifice Isaac as proof of his obedience to God. With a heavy heart Abraham agreed, but at the last moment God intervened and, praising Abraham for his faithfulness, spared Isaac and ordered Abraham to sacrifice a ram instead.

Isaac had twin sons – Jacob and Esau. Jacob had a dream one night in which he saw angels climbing a ladder into heaven and heard God promising him and his family the land on which they slept. Many years later Jacob met a stranger who challenged Jacob to wrestle with him through the night. The stranger revealed himself as another angel of God, and told Jacob that from now on he would be called Israel, which means 'one who strives with God'. The twelve tribes that formed the nation of Israel (*see* page 88) are said to have descended from Jacob's (Israel's) twelve sons.

Above As a sign of obedience, God commanded Abraham to sacrifice his son Isaac. At the last moment, when He was sure of Abraham's faithfulness, God intervened and spared Isaac.

Left Isaiah and the other prophets of the Hebrew Bible criticized immoral and ungodly behaviour. They constantly challenged people – even those in power – to walk the path of righteousness.

"Behold, I have set the land before you: go in and possess the land which the Lord swore unto your fathers, Abraham, Isaac and Jacob."

Deuteronomy 1:8

Moses and David

Moses is the next major figure who shaped the Jewish faith. With God's help he led the Israelites out of their slavery in Egypt, laid the foundations of the Hebrew nation and gave the people laws for worship and daily life. Once in the Promised Land the Israelites submitted themselves to the authority of anointed kings, who they hoped would rule over them justly according to God's laws. Their first great king was David, a warrior and musician who is credited with writing some of the Psalms – the sacred hymns or songs of the Hebrew Bible.

The prophets

Over the years, the kings and the people ignored God's teaching and were criticized for their bad behaviour by the prophets. Isaiah was a prophet of Judah in the 8th century BCE, at a time when some of the rich people were lazy in their worship and unjust to the poor. Isaiah told them that God would punish Judah if they did not improve their ways. Jeremiah was a gloomy, pessimistic prophet who foretold the destruction of Jerusalem. Other minor prophets spoke on similar themes: that faithfulness to God and a life of holiness are the most important things, and the consequences of sin and disobedience can be severe.

Above Jacob, who was later renamed Israel, had a dream of angels ascending a ladder to heaven. This painting is from the Christian Lambeth Bible (c.1140–50).

95

THE TEMPLE

At the back of the Temple there were steps that led to the Holy of Holies, where the Ark of the Covenant was kept.

Aﬆer King David turned Jerusalem into a great city, his son Solomon built the first Temple and established Jerusalem as the geographical and spiritual capital of his kingdom.

The Ark of the Covenant
At the core of the Temple was the Holy of Holies, the sanctuary where the Ark of the Covenant, a chest containing the Ten Commandments, was placed. The chest was carried by the ancient Israelites as they wandered through the desert towards the Promised Land, and it was their most precious possession. The Temple gave it a permanent home. So sacred were the Ark and its contents that only the High Priest could enter the sanctuary, and only once a year, on the Day of Atonement.

Building the Temple
The construction of the Temple is described in detail in the Book of Kings. The wood is said to have come from the cedar trees of Lebanon, or from fir and olive groves, and was carved with tiny flowers to form the floor, walls and roof beams. The stone structure was, in fact, carved elsewhere and assembled on site so that the sound of hammers and chisels would not disturb the sacred place. Construction of the Temple ('house' in the Hebrew Bible) was proof that the Jews were serving God who, in return, would bless them. Precious stones and metals were used in the construction, and even the hinges of the door leading to the Holy of Holies were made from gold.

Left This view of Jerusalem shows the Dome of the Rock and the Western (Wailing) Wall in the foreground.

Before they were sacrificed, lambs were washed in wheeled basins of water.

Below The Temple, built by King Solomon, was the spiritual centre of Jerusalem and of the kingdom. It was not just one building, but a series of buildings ringed by courtyards. The outer courtyard was open to everyone, including non-Jews (gentiles), but the rest of the space was reserved for Jews only. The inner courtyard of the priests is shown here.

Temple worship

Temple worship was extremely ritualistic and involved sacrifice and elaborate rites performed by priests. Later, some of the priests were criticized for putting the form of the ritual above the content of God's message. From the start, the prophets realized that no amount of sacrifice or incense would compensate for ungodly behaviour and, if people sinned against God or other people by lying, stealing or killing, God would punish them.

Above The largest remaining section of the Temple Mount is the Western Wall. Jews come here to say their prayers, facing the Wall and bowing ritually.

Destruction of the Temple

The Temple was destroyed in 586BCE, rebuilt after the Babylonian exile and extended under King Herod the Great, before its final destruction in 70CE. Today, the remaining Western Wall is the most sacred site in the Jewish world. Jews recite their prayers at the Wall or write them down on slips of paper that they insert into the cracks between the stones. The Western Wall is sometimes called the Wailing Wall because of the cries of devout Jews lamenting the destruction of the Temple. Traditionally, it is said that when the Messiah comes the Temple will be built again and that God's Kingdom of righteousness will come to Earth. When the Temple was finally destroyed, temple worship came to an end and the synagogue took its place.

Sacrificial lambs were roasted at the altar. To this day, a lamb shankbone is eaten on Passover in commemoration of this ritual sacrifice.

JEWISH WORSHIP

With the destruction of the Temple in 70CE, worship gradually centred on the synagogue, which originally meant 'meeting-place'. Worship, or *avodah* in Hebrew, implies service to the Creator and was referred to by the ancient rabbis as 'the service of the heart', that is to say, something done willingly and joyfully to give thanks for the divine gift of life.

Synagogue worship

Devout Jews attend the synagogue three times a day, in the morning, afternoon and evening – in a pattern that recalls the now vanished ritual of the Temple. In the morning and evening they recite the *Shema*. This is a group of three readings from the Torah, beginning with the words, "Hear O Israel, the Lord is our God, the Lord is One." The *Shema* is the basic affirmation of the Jewish faith.

For a full orthodox service to take place, ten men need to be present – a minimum requirement for communal worship, known as a *minyan*. At the heart of the service is a series of blessings called the *Amidah*, which are recited with the congregation standing. In the Orthodox tradition, women worship separately from the men, either in a space screened off from them or in a gallery above. Liberal Judaism is different. Men, women and children worship together.

Above *A child lights the candles of a* menorah, *a branched candlestick, used to celebrate Chanukah.*

The day of rest

The focal-point of the week is the Sabbath (*Shabbat*) the day of rest that the Ten Commandments decree should be kept holy. This is a day of worship centred on the synagogue and the home. The Sabbath begins on Friday evening at sunset, and the whole household will sit down for the family meal which ushers it in.

Right *The* Shabbat *meal has preserved Jewish identity. Here the blessing of wine and bread is made at the Sabbath table.*

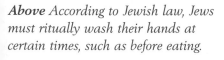

Above According to Jewish law, Jews must ritually wash their hands at certain times, such as before eating.

Below When praying in the synagogue, male Jews cover their heads with skull-caps as a mark of respect.

An act of worship

The beginning of the Sabbath is marked by the lighting of candles and is followed by a special meal. A blessing is made over the wine and bread, and the family sits down together to eat in commemoration of the creation of the world and the deliverance of the people of Israel out of slavery in Egypt. The family meal is an act of worship in itself – when the food is blessed, the table becomes an altar, emphasizing its importance as a spiritual focus. This domestic event has kept the Jewish identity intact in the most hostile circumstances.

The Torah gives practical instructions for observing the Sabbath. No work is permitted and no food may be cooked – although an exception is made to all these rules if someone's life is in danger. The definition of 'work' is very strict and even switching on a light qualifies. Many Jews have time switches fitted to allow electric appliances to come on automatically during the Sabbath. Jews do not consider these restrictions to be an inconvenience. Rather, they see them as a liberation from the working week and an opportunity to spend time at home with the entire family in worship, study or conversation. Orthodox Jews tend to interpret the rules more strictly than non-Orthodox Jews.

STUDYING THE LAW

The Hebrew Bible is not a book like any other. Many Jews believe it contains all there is to know in order to live a godly life. In particular, they base their lives on the revealed word of God, said to have been handed down in the form of the Torah on Mount Sinai. The Torah, as we have seen, comprises the first five books of the Hebrew Bible and contains 613 commandments, or *mitzvot*, which pious Jews must seek to study, to understand and to follow.

The tradition of scholarship

Study of these texts, which has exercised the minds of the most brilliant scholars in Jewish history, is the work of a lifetime, but every Jew is expected to spend some time studying the Torah. From an early age children are taught what the commandments are and are shown, through study and example, how to carry them out. At first they learn from their parents in the home, then from their teachers at the synagogue. Boys may also go to a *yeshiva*, or religious academy, where they will study the scriptures into their early twenties. Although study and debate are intense, the atmosphere is relaxed and informal. Orthodox women are generally not expected to study the Torah. Their religious duty is primarily to care for the home and raise children. Girls are admitted to colleges that follow a more liberal tradition and some go on to become rabbis themselves – although women rabbis are not recognized by the Orthodox community.

Above Elaborately decorated cases are used to house the Torah scrolls. The decoration does not include any human figures – in obedience to the commandment not to make a graven image.

Oral tradition

Throughout Jewish history the Torah has been discussed endlessly and from the earliest times interpretations have been handed down by word of mouth to the next generation. In about the 2nd century CE, Rabbi Judah ('the Prince') brought the oral traditions together in a written collection known as the *Mishnah*.

Left This female rabbi is using a yad, *or pointer, to read from the Torah. The text of the scrolls is never touched directly. The yad is used both to protect it, and as a sign of its sanctity.*

> "Behold, I set before you this day a blessing and a curse. A blessing if ye obey the commandments of the Lord your God and a curse if ye will not obey the commandments."
>
> Deuteronomy 12:27–28
> Exodus 20:2–3

In parallel with this, another volume of commentary was being prepared. The *Midrash* is a collection of sermons, stories and parables (*Aggadah*) told by rabbis to explain the Torah. Between 200 and 500CE, the *Mishnah* received its own commentary (known as the *Gemara*, or completion). Together these formed one enormous collection known as the Talmud, a comprehensive commentary on Jewish religious law (*Halakah*) that forms the backbone of a Jew's scholarly and religious life. It is said that in the life hereafter Jews are rewarded with an eternity in the presence of Moses himself, discussing the finer points of the Torah.

Reverence for the Torah

While the Talmud and other commentaries are regarded as books like any others, the Torah scrolls are given a special religious status. When a service is over the scrolls are carefully rolled up and replaced in a case, which is often richly decorated. Conditions of life have changed since the time of Moses, who could not have imagined a world of high technology, transplant surgery, genetic engineering or space flight. But many Jews still believe that the basic laws of 3,000 years ago can be reinterpreted to apply to every circumstance today.

Left Scholarship is very important in the Jewish tradition. Study of the Talmud begins at an early age.

THE JEWISH CALENDAR

The Jewish New Year begins with Rosh Hashanah, a time to look back on mistakes made during the previous year and to resolve to do better in the year ahead. A ram's horn (a *shofar*) is blown, and this produces a raw, piercing sound that calls all sinners to repentance. The Rosh Hashanah festival is the annual commemoration of God's creation and a reminder that all our deeds will be judged. Traditionally, Jews eat apples dipped in honey to wish each other a sweet New Year. The next ten days are then set aside for serious reflection and preparation for Yom Kippur – the most sacred day of the religious calendar.

The Day of Atonement

Yom Kippur is the culmination of the ten days of self-examination that began at Rosh Hashanah. In ancient times, this was the one day in the year when the high priest made a sacrifice to atone for the sins of the people and entered the Holy of Holies in the Jerusalem Temple, where the Ten Commandments had been placed. Today, sacrifice is no longer carried out and, instead, the Day of Atonement is focused on the synagogue, where a day-long service is held, accompanied by a 25-hour fast. When the congregation has admitted its sins, prayers are said for forgiveness. Yom Kippur is regarded as an annual opportunity for spiritual renewal.

Above *For the festival of Sukkot, these Jewish school children are building temporary shelters (tabernacles or booths) as a reminder of the years that the Israelites spent wandering in the desert with only tents for shelter.*

Left *A family lights the Chanukah candles recalling the re-dedication of the Temple in 165BCE after it had been desecrated by the Syrians.*

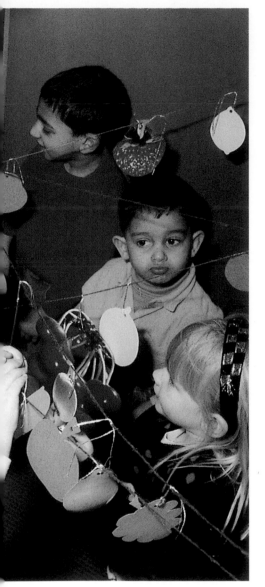

The Feast of Tabernacles

Five days after Yom Kippur, the Feast of Tabernacles, or Sukkot, takes place, when Jews remember how God provided for the Children of Israel as they wandered in the desert for 40 years before arriving in the Promised Land. As a reminder of their time in the wilderness, when they had only tents to sleep in, Jews construct temporary shelters (tabernacles or booths) at home or in the synagogue. They may eat, study or even sleep in them. At the end of Sukkot there is a synagogue service known as Simchat Torah, or Rejoicing in the Law. The scrolls are paraded around the synagogue, to the accompaniment of joyful singing and dancing.

> **"Love the Lord your God and keep ... his laws and his commandments always."**
>
> Deuteronomy 11:1

Remembering the past

Chanukah is a winter festival, but it celebrates more than just a seasonal cycle. It reminds Jews of the period in their history (165BCE) when they fought the Greek influences that threatened their identity and the purity of their Temple. Judas Maccabaeus, a member of the Hasmonean family, led a revolt against those who had desecrated the Temple. According to legend there was enough oil in the temple lamp to last for one day, but miraculously it burned for eight days, at the end of which Judas Maccabaeus re-dedicated the Temple. In public and private ceremonies Jews celebrate the festival by lighting candles on an eight-branched *menorah*. A ninth branch holds the 'servant candle' from which the rest are lit – one on the first day, two on the second, three on the third and so on, until the candlestick is ablaze with light.

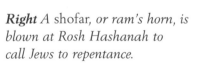

Right A shofar, *or ram's horn, is blown at Rosh Hashanah to call Jews to repentance.*

JEWISH TRADITION

Passover, or Pesach in Hebrew, recalls the story of the Exodus from Egypt. It takes its name from the last of the ten plagues that persuaded the pharaoh to set the Israelites free. First the Nile River turned to blood, then there was a plague of frogs, a plague of gnats and a plague of flies. Next the Egyptian cattle died, and the people were afflicted with boils. After hailstones and a plague of locusts, followed by a three-day period of darkness, the most devastating of the plagues descended. The Angel of Death 'passed over' the children of Israel but the first-born son of every Egyptian died. The pharaoh agreed to release the Israelites, who left in such a hurry that they were unable to let the bread they had prepared for their journey rise. As a result only unleavened bread (bread without yeast) can be eaten for the week of Passover. A ritual meal is prepared of foods that symbolize the flight from Egypt. Traditionally, the youngest child present asks, "Why is this night different from all other nights?", and the father tells the story of the Exodus.

Shavuot (originally a harvest festival) is celebrated 50 days after the second day of Passover and it recalls the handing over of the Torah to Moses on Mount Sinai. The Ten Commandments are read out in the synagogue, which is often decorated with flowers and fruit to celebrate the first fruits of the season.

Above Passover is as important today as it was in the time of Moses. The symbolism of the meal, here depicted in a 15th-century manuscript, has remained unchanged.

The Festival of Lots

Purim – the Festival of Lots – is one of the minor festivals. It commemorates the victory of Esther and her uncle Mordechai over Haman, a minister of the Persian Emperor who threatened to exterminate the Jewish people and cast lots (*purim*) to decide on which day he should carry out his threat.

THE SEDER MEAL

The ritual Passover meal is known as *seder*. Bitter herbs recall slavery, an egg and a lamb shankbone commemorate ritual sacrifice, saltwater symbolizes the tears of the Israelites and a mixture of nuts, cinnamon and wine represents the mortar they were forced to mix for the pharaoh's building. The unleavened bread – a dry cracker known as *Matzah* – is the bread of affliction.

Right A Jewish bride and groom celebrate their wedding under the huppah*(canopy) which is a symbol of God's sheltering, protective power.*

Below At the age of 13, a boy comes of age and becomes a Bar Mitzvah, *or Son of the Commandment. During prayer orthodox Jews wear* tefillin *on their head and arms. These are small boxes containing scriptural texts.*

Rites of passage

As descendants of the patriarch Abraham, Jews belong to an ancient family, and it is as a family that they mark the great life-cycle events. These begin shortly after birth, when boys are circumcised as a mark of God's covenant with Abraham. Girls are blessed. Jewish boys come of age when they are 13, and at a special service marking the transition into adulthood, they become a *Bar Mitzvah*, or Son of the Commandment. Girls come of age when they are 12 and become a *Bat Mitzvah*, or Daughter of the Commandment.

It is usually hoped that men and women will find a marriage partner from within the community because 'marrying out' is often seen as a rejection of Jewish identity. Weddings are very festive occasions, with the whole community joining in the celebrations. Couples marry beneath a *huppah*, or canopy, a survival of the ancient bridal bower in which newlyweds used to be secluded after the ceremony. The groom breaks a glass beneath his foot – a reminder that life is fragile.

Jewish funerals usually take place within 24 hours of death. Relatives make a small tear in their garment as a mark of mourning and the deceased's children recite the *Kaddish*, a prayer which is a mark of mourning but also an affirmation of life.

DIVISIONS IN JUDAISM

Throughout their long and often troubled history the Jews have tried to keep their identity as a people intact. However, being part of a family, they have sometimes had bitter family quarrels that have caused division among them. The principle theological divisions are between Orthodox and Progressive Judaism.

Orthodox Judaism

Orthodox Judaism sees itself as the only true and authentic Judaism, maintaining an unbroken tradition stretching back to Moses. Orthodox Jews cannot keep to all the 613 commandments because many relate to the era of the Temple, which has ceased to exist, but those they do keep have to be followed, however inconvenient this may be in the modern world. At the end of the 19th century a modern Orthodoxy emerged, encouraging Jews to break out of the ghetto (the section of a city to which Jews were restricted) and take part in the intellectual, political and artistic life of the wider community while still remaining true to the Torah. It was now possible for a Jew to mix with mainstream society at school, university or work and still be true to his or her Biblical inheritance.

Below Ethiopian Jews, or Falashas, airlifted to Israel in 1985, were said by some not to be authentically Jewish. Many underwent 're-conversion' ceremonies to reaffirm their faith.

Hasidism

Hasidism is a branch of Orthodoxy that lays great stress on tradition. Members are wrongly described as 'ultra-orthodox' – a better word is 'ultra-traditionalist', because they follow the traditions and styles of dress of late 18th-century Poland and Germany. They view non-Jewish thinking with suspicion and worship in a way that stresses enthusiasm, passion and devotion. The best-known group is that of the Lubavitch, which thrives in New York.

Because the demands made on them are great, traditionalist groups tend to live in the same area, working in Jewish businesses, mixing with Jewish friends and living an ordered and disciplined life centred on the home and the synagogue.

Reform Judaism

Also known as Progressive or Liberal Judaism, the Reform movement began in Germany in the early 19th century and spread in particular to the United States, where it is the dominant form of Judaism today. Followers do not believe that the Torah was 'handed over' complete to Moses, but that it was written by humans with God's inspiration. For them, the attempt to work out God's will is an ongoing process. Worship is less ritualistic and their approach to women is more inclusive. They are prepared, for example, to ordain women as rabbis. Converts to Reform Judaism are not considered Jewish by Orthodox groups.

Above The ultra-traditionalist community of Mea Sharim in Jerusalem keeps itself apart from mainstream society and retains its own distinct identity.

Zionism

Jerusalem was also known as the City of Zion, the name lent to the modern Zionist movement founded by an Austrian Jew, Theodor Herzl, in the late 19th century. He believed at first that Jews could flourish in any country, but changed his mind when he saw how deep-rooted anti-semitism was. He therefore suggested establishing an independent homeland in Palestine. This mainly secular movement was opposed by Reform Jews, who felt that absorption into the wider society was healthier for Jewish culture, and also by religious conservatives, who felt that no return to the land of Israel was possible until the Messiah had come. In 1948, the state of Israel came into being, but while its legitimacy is constantly being questioned by the Palestinians, it has offered Jews around the world a haven from persecution.

Right Modern Zionism championed the idea of an independent homeland for the Jews. These children carry the Israeli flag.

CHRISTIANITY: AN INTRODUCTION

T he founder of Christianity was a Jew named Jesus, a teacher and healer who lived some 2,000 years ago in Palestine. His life, death and resurrection became the basis for a religion practised by almost a third of the world's population.

Early ministry
The details of Jesus' life and ministry are found in the four Gospels of what Christians call the New Testament of the Bible. They accept the authority of the Hebrew Bible (for them, the Old Testament), but believe it was superseded by a new covenant with God, of which Jesus was the living sign. Jesus himself said he had not come to alter the scriptures, but to fulfil them. He taught by example, living a simple and selfless life based on love. Christian love has two elements – love of God and love of other people. Despite the cruelty sometimes committed in the name of Christianity, this is the basis of the faith.

Below Jesus chose 12 apostles, or disciples, to help him spread the word of God (the gospel or 'good news'). They believed him to be the Messiah ('anointed one') foretold in the Hebrew scriptures. On the night before his death, Jesus ate a final meal with his disciples – 'the Last Supper'.

> ## "I and my Father are one."
> John 10:30

Life and death

In his day, Jesus' teaching was controversial and brought him into conflict not only with the Romans occupying the country but also with the Jewish religious leaders. They considered him to be a false messiah who refused to accept the rulings of the religious authorities – an offence for which the penalty could be death. Jesus was thought to be a threat to the stability of the state, so he was handed over to the Romans and crucified – a death that involved nailing him to a cross and leaving him there to die.

Above The Eucharist, also known as Holy Communion, commemorates the Last Supper and is central to Christian worship.

Below From its origins in the Mediterranean, Christianity has spread all over the world. Here Christians remember events leading up to Jesus' resurrection at the Festival of Holy Week in Peru.

Resurrection and salvation

The circumstances surrounding Jesus' death are of as much importance as his ministry. The Bible says that, three days after his crucifixion, Jesus rose from the dead and appeared again to his disciples. This miraculous resurrection was taken as proof that he was indeed the Son of God and that his message of salvation was true.

Spreading the word

Christianity has always been a missionary religion that aims to convert people to its way of life and its message. During the last 2,000 years missionary movements have spread it all over the world. One of the principal figures responsible for spreading Christianity after Christ's death was Paul of Tarsus, a Jew and a Roman citizen who converted to Christianity after seeing a blinding flash of light on the road to Damascus. While some members of this newly formed sect saw Christianity as another branch of Judaism to be reserved for Jews only, Paul argued that it was a universal religion that should be taken to every corner of the world and freely offered to humankind.

THE DEVELOPMENT OF CHRISTIANITY

From its origins as a simple community of 12 disciples who owned few possessions and shared everything, Christianity has become a global religion of great complexity. The Church owns land, buildings, churches, cathedrals and even television stations and satellites to further the Kingdom of God on Earth.

The Holy Spirit descends

The initial impulse to take the Gospel to every part of the world came at Pentecost and is described in the second chapter of the Acts of the Apostles. The disciples were sitting together deciding how best to spread God's word now that Jesus was no longer with them when suddenly the room was filled with "a rushing mighty wind and cloven tongues of fire". They were filled with the Holy Spirit, which enabled them to speak in other languages, and which prompted them to spread the faith far and wide.

The Holy Roman Empire

In his epistles (letters) Paul describes the community life of the early Christians, who were a minority religion persecuted by the Roman Empire. It was not until Emperor Constantine converted and made Christianity the state religion that their fortunes improved. However, official recognition was a mixed blessing because it became associated with powerful empires that used force to expand their territory.

Above Between 46CE and 62CE, Paul travelled around the Mediterranean on missionary journeys. The black line shows his first journey (46–48CE), the green line his second journey (49–52CE) and the red line his third journey (53–57CE). The blue line shows how Paul's fourth journey (59–62CE) took him as far as Rome.

Below Peter the Hermit, riding on a donkey, addresses Crusaders on their way to recapture the Holy Land from Islamic occupation in 1096CE.

Right In the Orthodox tradition, icons, or devotional pictures of holy figures – here Mary and the baby Jesus – are important in worship. Some Western Catholics in the 11th century (and even some Christians today) viewed them with great suspicion, comparing their use to idol worship. This was one of the factors leading to the great split.

Below The medieval cathedrals are monuments to the intensity of Christian faith in the Middle Ages. This picture, by a French artist of the 15th century, shows the building of a cathedral.

Division and dissent

As Christianity grew, so, too, did its divisions. The first major split was the 'Great Schism' of 1054, which resulted in a division between the Western Catholic Church based in Rome and the Eastern Orthodox Church based in Constantinople (now Istanbul in Turkey). Fifty years later, a series of religious and military expeditions known as the Crusades was mounted. These were organized by Christian forces in an attempt to conquer the Holy Land and liberate the holy sites from Muslim control.

Although the Middle Ages, which lasted until the 15th century CE, produced magnificent Christian art and architecture, there was deep unrest. Abuse of religious power, immoral behaviour by priests, bishops and popes and a general neglect of the essentials of the Christian faith were common. Reform was needed.

Change and reform

The most important of the reforming groups was led by the German theologian Martin Luther (1483–1546), who opposed the Church's sale of 'indulgences'. These were 'pardons', which were handed over by the priests in exchange for cash. They were supposed to release people from their sins and so allow them to buy their way into heaven. Luther condemned this practice and went further still. He stressed 'justification by faith' and argued that no amount of good deeds would save people from sin. Forgiveness came only through faith in Jesus. The Lutheran group and other similar movements are known collectively as the Reformation. They upset the power structures within the Church and split it in two – the Roman Catholic Church, and the breakaway Protestant Church, which itself divided into many different denominations.

THE LIFE OF JESUS

Despite the many divisions within Christianity, all believers try to live a life based on that of their founder, Jesus Christ. Accounts of the life of Jesus Christ were passed on by word of mouth and it was not until some 35 years after his death that they were first written down in story form. The first account was in Mark's Gospel, on which the gospels of Matthew and Luke were partly based. These, known as the Synoptic Gospels (accounts describing Christ's ministry from the same general point of view), were joined by a fourth, John's Gospel, which is different in tone and concentrates less on the life than on the interpretation of the message.

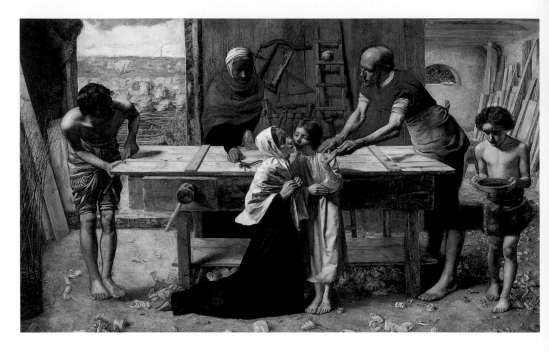

Above Christ in the House of His Parents, *painted in 1849–1850 by Sir John Everett Millais, depicts the boyhood of Jesus as a carpenter's son.*

The life of Christ

The Gospels say that Jesus was born of the Virgin Mary, who conceived him through the power of the Holy Spirit. He was born in Bethlehem and brought up by Mary and her husband Joseph, a carpenter, in Nazareth. When Jesus was about 30 years old his ministry began with his baptism by John the Baptist at the River Jordan. After this he went into the desert to fast and prepare himself spiritually for the work ahead. After 40 days in the wilderness he was tempted by the devil, but resisted. His ministry lasted only three years, but in that time he became a charismatic teacher and healer, impressing people with his goodness, gentleness and strength. Jesus was tolerant of people's failings and slow to condemn.

Left In this painting by Piero Della Francesca (c.1419–1492) John the Baptist baptizes Christ at the start of his ministry. The dove is the traditional sign of the Holy Spirit.

Above One of Jesus' most famous miracles was the feeding of the 5,000 (Matthew 14:13–21). A crowd of people had come to hear Jesus preach and were amply fed with only five loaves and two fishes.

"I am the door; by me, if any man enter in he shall be saved".

John 10:9

Performing miracles

The Bible says that Jesus performed many miracles, such as turning water into wine at the wedding feast at Cana (John 2:1–11). Miracles are not magic tricks done to impress an audience – in Christian thinking they are spiritual signs that show a truth about God's kingdom. The wine is a symbol of the abundance of life that believers in Christ receive.

A friend to all

Jesus was frequently seen in the company of people rejected by society. In particular he healed lepers, who were considered unclean by the Temple priests. Jesus appealed very much to ordinary people because he spoke in a way they could easily understand. His method was to use parables, that is to say, simple stories to illustrate profound spiritual truths. Among the most famous are the parables of the Good Samaritan, the Unjust Judge, the Great Feast, and the Labourers in the Vineyard. All this was a direct challenge to the Temple authorities, who began to consider how they could get rid of him. One of the last things Jesus did before his arrest was to eat a meal with his disciples. At the 'Last Supper', Jesus said that the bread and the wine would be a memorial to his body and his blood and that the meal should be symbolically recreated by his followers in his memory. The Gospel of Matthew ends with Jesus' promise, "I am with you always even unto the end of the world."

113

THE CRUCIFIXION

The crucifixion of Christ and his resurrection from the dead are at the core of Christian belief. Jesus' anguish as he approached death and his agony on the cross with nails through his hands and feet, as described in the Gospels, have come to be called the Passion.

The first covenant

The Old Testament Book of Genesis says that God created humans in the form of Adam and Eve and made an earthly paradise known as the Garden of Eden. But Adam and Eve rebelled and were cast out of paradise – a doctrine known as the Fall. From then on, the long process began to liberate people from sin and to restore God's kingdom on Earth. God's first attempt after the Fall involved a covenant with Noah. God promised that Noah and his family, plus two of every animal in creation, would be spared from a destructive flood by escaping on an ark (vast boat). But after the flood had subsided, humanity again returned to its wicked ways and worshipped false idols.

The second covenant

God's second covenant was with Abraham and the people of Israel (*see* page 88), but again the people sinned. Something urgent had to be done once and for all, so God decided to make what Christians believe is the ultimate sacrifice, to free creation from its wickedness: He sent His only Son, Jesus, to Earth knowing that he would die on the cross. With this supreme act of self-sacrifice Jesus, the promised Messiah, would save humanity from sin.

With the crucifixion and the resurrection Christians believe that God, through Christ, has ultimately broken the power of the devil and offered salvation to all those who want it.

Above In the top section Judas, one of the disciples, betrays Christ with a kiss. He was so ashamed that he later committed suicide. In the bottom section, Jesus is brought before Pilate.

Left Christ was made to carry his own cross to Golgotha and he was mocked by the people. In many parts of the world, this scene is re-enacted every Easter.

Above Jesus was stripped naked, beaten and crowned with thorns as a mocking reminder that he had claimed to be King of the Jews.

"And Jesus cried with a loud voice, and gave up the ghost."

Mark 15:37

The story of Christ's Passion
Jesus' claim to be the Messiah and his criticism of the Temple's empty rituals angered the religious authorities. At one point Jesus went into the Temple compound, overturned the moneychangers' tables and announced that they were turning the house of God into a marketplace. The chief priests feared that Jesus would destroy their authority and decided to have him arrested. They did a deal with one of his disciples, Judas Iscariot. In exchange for 30 pieces of silver, Judas agreed to betray Jesus. Jesus knew this and said so (Mark 14:18–21) at the Last Supper. He went to the Garden of Gethsemane to pray and to ask God to release him from his fate, but finally realized that God's will, not his own, had to be done.

As Jesus was about to leave the Garden of Gethsemane, he and his disciples were surrounded by soldiers. Judas Iscariot stepped forward and kissed Jesus – this was a pre-arranged signal to let the soldiers know whom to arrest. Jesus was tried before Pontius Pilate, the Roman governor, who found him guilty of no crime. However, he agreed to the mob's wishes and had Jesus crucified on a hill called Golgotha (the place of the skull) between two criminals.

After some hours on the cross Jesus died in agony with the words, "Father, into thy hands I commend my spirit" (Luke 23:46). Immediately there was an earthquake and part of the Temple was destroyed. Three days later the Bible says Jesus rose again from the dead and told his disciples that they should now spread the message of God's love for humankind and the hope of life after death.

THE TRINITY

Christians traditionally believe that Jesus Christ had a divine father (God) and an earthly mother (Mary). As a result they believe Christ to be both human and divine.

The Incarnation

The doctrine of the Incarnation (Latin *caro* meaning 'flesh') is summed up in statements at the beginning of John's Gospel: "In the beginning was the Word, and the Word was with God, and the Word was God … and the Word was made flesh." Christians understand the 'Word' to mean the divine plan underlying all Creation, a plan that is not separate from God Himself. The divine plan was revealed to humanity in the flesh and blood of one man, Jesus, who similarly is not separate from God Himself. Jesus is one with God. Father and Son are one.

The Holy Spirit

After his ascension into Heaven, Jesus was no longer visible in the world, but the Bible says he communicated with humanity through his Holy Spirit, which descended on the disciples at Pentecost. God, Christ and the Holy Spirit are known as the Trinity, or three beings in one God – God the Father, God the Son and God the Holy Spirit – rather than a collection of three gods. This idea has long been debated by Christians and they still fail to agree. A mainstream belief is that the Trinity represents three aspects of God, or three ways of knowing more about God's nature and purpose.

Above This painting, The Descent of the Holy Ghost, *is by Sandro Botticelli (c.1441–1510). In Christian doctrine the Trinity – Father, Son and Holy Spirit (or Ghost) – are thought of as three aspects of the one god.*

Left Masai women attend a Pentecostal service in Tanzania. Charismatic or Pentecostal Christians believe that the gifts of the Holy Spirit help them to heal the sick.*

Above In Christian imagery God often appears as a wise and powerful old man, a patriarch like Moses. This is how the artist Michelangelo portrayed God's creation of the first man on Earth, Adam.

Below The Lamb of God is a powerful symbol of Christian redemption. This picture of the lamb in heaven comes from a manuscript called the Lambeth Apocalypse (c.1260CE)

Knowing the unknowable

Christians believe that God is infinite and eternal and, as such, beyond human understanding. However, certain things *can* be known about the Creator – that He is a Father figure, for example, who cares for humanity as a father cares for his children, loving at all times but also occasionally strict. But other Christians say this description is not sufficient. They point to other imagery in the Bible that stresses the feminine side of God's nature, and even refer to God as 'Our Heavenly Father and Mother'.

The Lamb of God

Through the second person of the Trinity, Jesus Christ, Christians believe that other aspects of God's nature have been revealed. An image often used is that of the lamb. This has its origins in the Jewish tradition of sacrificing a lamb at Passover (*see* page 104), but in Christian thinking it means that God so loved the world that He was prepared to pay the ultimate price – the sacrifice of His only Son – to buy back (redeem) the world from the clutches of sin and death.

> **"There is one body and one spirit, one Lord, one faith, one baptism, one God and Father of all."**
>
> Ephesians IV:4–6

117

CHRISTIAN WORSHIP

Christian worship can take place anywhere and at any time, but it is usually carried out privately with prayers in the home, or publicly at church services attended by a congregation or community of believers. Worship takes many different forms. For example, it can be full of ceremony with priests and bishops dressed in colourful robes or vestments; or it can be a simple gathering of Christians meeting together for prayer at someone's house. There may be loud music with trumpets, organs, guitars and choirs, or there may be quiet meditation in the silence of a plain room. Jesus said that all that was needed for Christian worship to begin was the presence of people gathered together in his name.

In practice most Christians consider Sunday a special day to be set aside for worship in church. They meet to say prayers, sing hymns and hear extracts of the Bible. The priest or minister will deliver a sermon, or short talk designed to explain an aspect of the Christian life. After the service there might be Bible study or Sunday school classes in the church hall.

Above Christian prayer is essentially a conversation with God. Children are taught that, even though they cannot see him, Jesus is with them always.

The five themes

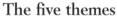

Christian worship focuses on five principal themes – adoration, praise, thanksgiving, repentance and petition. Adoration is the expression of the love that Christians believe is owed to God the Creator who sacrificed His only Son to save the world. Praise is the passionate celebration of God's splendour, power and majesty. Thanksgiving is the expression of gratitude for the gift of life. Repentance involves the confession of sin and the promise to be a better person, and petition is the equally human request for help in times of need.

Left A young girl lighting candles at a Catholic church service in Lithuania. Candles have always been important in Christian worship as a symbol of the light that Jesus brought into the world.

Below Singing hymns is a popular part of a Christian church service. The music is traditionally played on a organ and there is usually a choir to lead the congregration.

The Lord's Prayer

The New Testament contains the prayer that Jesus taught his followers to say, the Lord's Prayer. It is central to Christian worship in that it provides a model of prayer and tells believers what Christ himself considered important about relationships with God and with one another. It is sometimes asked why, if God knows all our needs already (Matthew 6:32), there is any need to pray at all. There are two answers to this. The first is simple: Christ prayed, so we should do so, too. The second answer is that God wants us to co-operate with Him, rather than expecting Him to do everything for us.

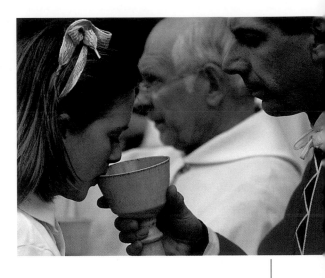

Above At Holy Communion, the priest or minister blesses the bread and wine and the worshippers receive them in memory of the body and blood of Christ.

Church worship

There is a carefully prepared structure to most church worship, which is known as the liturgy. This lays down the form of the prayers, the order of service and the choice of readings. In some traditions (notably the Orthodox), this structure has not changed for generations and people go to a church service knowing exactly what to expect. In more modern forms of worship (especially within the Evangelical tradition), the whole service seems more informal and spontaneous. Members of the congregation are encouraged to take part – either in the preparation of the liturgy or in the leading of the prayers. In some (nowadays rare) Roman Catholic services the entire service takes place in Latin. But whatever form Christian worship takes, human beings are gathered together in friendship to offer praise and thanks to God.

THE SACRAMENTS

C hristian worship often focuses on scenes from Christ's earthly ministry and uses them symbolically to mark important turning points in people's lives.

The sacrament of baptism

The first of these is the sacrament of baptism. A sacrament is defined as 'an outward and visible sign of an inward and spiritual grace'. Baptism marks admission to the Christian Church and recalls the moment, at the beginning of Christ's ministry, when he was baptized by John the Baptist in the waters of the River Jordan. Today, there are two forms of this ritual – infant and adult baptism – and there is debate as to which form is preferable. Some say that admission to the Church should be delayed until people are old enough to make this commitment for themselves. Others argue that people should be welcomed into the community of believers as soon as possible, shortly after birth.

> **"You are all the children of God by faith in Christ Jesus."**
>
> Galatians III:26–8

Above *In some traditions, baptism is considered such an important rite of passage that only those who have made a mature decision to become a Christian may be baptized – usually by total immersion in the water.*

In most churches there is a font (ceremonial bowl) or pool set aside for baptism. Baptism with water has its origins in early purification rites, but in Christianity it is used as a visible sign that the child is being born again into a new life in Christ. Normally the mother and father choose godparents, who take part in the ceremony and promise to look after the child's spiritual development.

Adult baptism frequently involves total immersion in the water, which symbolizes purification from the sins of Adam and Eve and the beginning of a new life in obedience to Christ. The minister and helpers stand waist deep in the water and, after prayers, tip the person backwards and totally immerse him or her for a second or two.

Right *Children are baptized by a priest or minister, who welcomes them into the Christian Church by pouring water over their foreheads.*

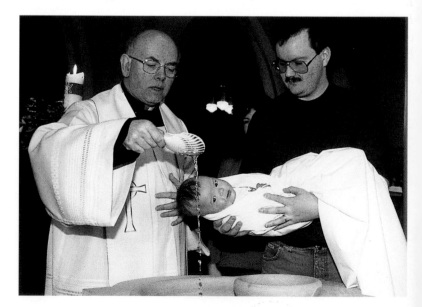

Confirmation

People who have been baptized as infants often want to affirm or renew their commitment to the faith in a public way. They do this by confirmation, which takes place after instruction by a priest or minister. In Protestant and Catholic churches the confirmation is usually carried out by a bishop, who lays hands on the person's head to signify that Christ's living Spirit is being passed on.

Above A marriage in church is both a joyful event and a solemn exchange of vows. Here a Orthodox Christian wedding takes place in Sofia, Bulgaria.

The Eucharist

Also known as Holy Communion, the Lord's Supper, the Mass, and the Divine Liturgy, the Eucharist is at the heart of Christian worship. It commemorates the Last Supper when Christ told his disciples to eat bread (his body) and drink wine (his blood) in remembrance of him. In some traditions, Communion, during which the congregation is given a small piece of bread or a wafer (a host) and a sip of wine from a goblet or chalice, is reserved for those who have been confirmed. In the Roman Catholic tradition, it is believed that during this sacrament the bread and the wine actually become the body and the blood of Christ – a doctrine known as transubstantiation.

Below Full members of the church take Holy Communion in remembrance of the Last Supper. Here Mass is being celebrated in Zimbabwe.

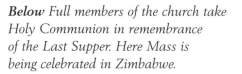

Holy matrimony

During the sacrament of holy matrimony the bride and groom vow to remain faithful to each other until death. Marriages are happy occasions and call to mind the first of Jesus' miracles at the wedding feast in Cana, where he turned water into wine (*see* page 113). Marriage is also a symbol of Christ's union with his Church.

CHRISTMAS

Christmas is the time when Christians remember and celebrate the birth of Jesus Christ. It is a happy time when people give presents in memory of the joy God brought to the world in the form of His only son.

'Lighten our darkness'

In the early days of Christianity, Easter was *the* central Christian festival and it was not until 400 years after the birth of Christ that Christmas became an official Christian observance. Before that time there where many folk or pagan midwinter festivals, when people celebrated the fact that the worst of winter was over and that warmer weather was not far away. The early Church modified these existing festivals for its own purpose and gave them a Christian significance. They became an opportunity to celebrate the birth of Christ as 'the Light of the World'.

Preparing for Christmas

Preparations begin four Sundays before Christmas Day at the start of Advent, which means 'coming'. During this time Christians think about what the arrival of Christ means to them personally as well as to the whole human race. Children are often given an Advent Calendar so they can count down to Christmas Day.

Above *Many artists have portrayed Christ as a light coming into the darkness of the world. This painting, entitled* The Light of the World, *is by William Holman Hunt (1827–1910).*

THE NATIVITY

Only two of the New Testament Gospels, Matthew and Luke, tell the story of Christ's birth, or Nativity. The stories are not the same, but some of the details overlap. The traditional picture that Christians have is a mixture of the two accounts. The baby Jesus was born in a manger, or feeding trough, in a stable surrounded by farm animals. His parents, Mary and Joseph, had been turned away from the inn where they intended to stay because there was no room for them. To mark the event, Three Wise Men, or Magi, were guided by a star to the manger. They laid gifts of gold, frankincense and myrrh at the infant's feet. Children frequently re-enact the scene in school Nativity plays.

Above The presents brought by the Magi are symbolic. The gold suggests Christ's majesty as a king and Messiah. Frankincense and myrrh are sweet-smelling resins from the bark of certain trees. They also have healing properties, which make them useful for embalming (preserving) dead bodies.

"Magi came from the east to Jerusalem and asked, 'Where is the one who has been born King of the Jews?'"

(Matthew 2:1-2)

In most Christian traditions Christmas Day is celebrated on December 25 – though the Orthodox Christmas is on January 6. Homes are decorated with holly and ivy, plants that symbolize Christ's eternal presence in the world. Christmas carols that tell of Christ's birth are sung, and in many churches Mass is held at midnight on Christmas Eve so that worshippers can enter into the joy of Christmas from the beginning of Christmas Day.

Christmas in the West has become very commercialized, but even some of the secular elements have religious roots. Father Christmas, or Santa Claus, is based on the patron saint of children, St Nicholas, who is traditionally associated with the giving of presents.

Despite the pressure to spend money and to 'eat, drink and be merry', many people still catch a glimpse of the pure joy that Christ's birth is believed to have brought to the world.

The Three Wise Men
The Festival of Epiphany in early January celebrates the arrival of the Three Wise Men, who were the first gentiles (non-Jews) to see Christ. This shows that Christ's message – peace on Earth and goodwill to all humanity – is a universal one and that salvation is open to anyone who believes in him.

CELEBRATING EASTER

The Easter season is the most important time of year for Christian believers and a time of both sadness and joy. On Good Friday they remember the Crucifixion when Jesus Christ was put to death on the cross. On Easter Sunday, they remember the Resurrection – the day he rose from the dead.

The 40 days before Easter is a special time for Christian prayer and contemplation. The period is known as Lent and people deny themselves pleasures such as sweets. The story of Easter is told in the New Testament. Jesus claimed to be the Son of God and was considered a threat by the Jewish and Roman authorities. On Good Friday, he was crucified on a hill outside Jerusalem on the order of Pontius Pilate. Later that day, his followers took his body and buried it in a tomb – a cave sealed with a stone. On the third day, celebrated now as Easter Sunday, women followers went to visit the tomb. They discovered that the stone had been rolled away. The body of Jesus had gone and in its place were two angels who said, "Why do you look for the living among the dead? He is not here, but has risen."

Above In many faiths, the egg is a symbol of life. This Easter egg, studded with jewels, was made for the Russian tsar Nicholas II.

Above Jesus Christ rises from the dead and steps out of the tomb on Easter Day. Although this Italian painting is more than 500 years old, the scene is still central to Christian belief.

Right On the night before Easter every year, Christians at the Church of the Holy Sepulchre in Jerusalem celebrate the ceremony of 'new light' with candles. The church is a blaze of light as flares are passed from hand to hand.

Above Fish symbols, often associated with Christ, decorate this Ukrainian Easter egg.

"Fear not … I know that you seek Jesus who was crucified. He is not here. For he has risen …"

Matthew 28:5–6

To mark the joy of this event, Christians break their Lenten fast on Easter Sunday and celebrate with a feast. Holy Week and Easter have always been celebrated by Christians as a time to remember that God loves people so much that He sent His son, Jesus, to die for the world. As a result, Easter has always been a special time for the baptism of new Christians.

Even before Christian times, many people celebrated spring in a special way. It is the season when trees sprout leaves again, when nature is 'reborn' after the deadness of winter – just as Jesus rose from the dead. People held spring festivals, and many of their traditions carried over into the Christian Easter. The giving of Easter eggs, for example, goes back to pre-Christian times. The egg, from which a chick will be born, is a sign of fertility, a reminder that older generations die but younger ones will eventually take their place.

THE HISTORY OF EASTER BREAD

Special cakes are eaten at Easter. The hot cross bun (below left) bears the sign of the cross on which Jesus was crucified. The fruit and spices that are used to make the bun are a reminder of the happiness that his resurrection brings. For centuries, the people living in Frankfurt, Germany, ate pretzels (far right) at their very popular Easter fairs.

THE RELIGIOUS LIFE

In every religion there are individuals who feel drawn to a more intense form of spiritual experience. As a result some may feel a vocation (calling) to religious life and to an extra degree of Christian commitment.

The ordained ministry

To become priests or ministers, candidates have to persuade the Church that their commitment is genuine and that they are intellectually and temperamentally suited for ordination. In the Roman Catholic and Orthodox traditions only men can become priests. After selection they undergo several years of training, during which time they learn about the history and traditions of the Church, study the Bible and other books of Christian theology, and learn about the practical requirements of being a Christian leader. Once they have been ordained, they may be given a parish (a geographical area with its own church) where they will look after people's needs.

Monks and nuns

Some people feel called to take up the religious life as monks or nuns in monasteries or convents. They take three vows – of poverty, chastity and obedience – and live a very disciplined life, deliberately set apart from the outside world. There are many religious groups, or orders. Among the best known are the Dominicans, the Franciscans, the Benedictines, the Carmelites, the Cistercians and the Trappists. Some of these are enclosed, contemplative orders in which monks and nuns devote themselves to prayer and reflection in a community that is completely cut off from the outside world. Other orders have considerable contact with the world and work with people who need their help.

Above *St Francis lived a life of self-denial and was said to be very close to nature. Birds and animals felt safe in his presence and it is even said that they came to hear him preach.*

Right *Pilgrims were a familiar sight on the roads of Europe in the 15th century. Here, they are making their way to the cathedral at Santiago de Compostela in northern Spain.*

The first monasteries

The pattern of western monasticism was set by an Italian, St Benedict (*c*.480–550CE). At the age of 14, he became a hermit and his devotion to Christ's austere way of life attracted many followers. In the mid-6th century he established a monastery at Monte Casino, between Rome and Naples, and drew up what is known as the Rule of St Benedict. This involves a strict timetable of study, prayer and manual work within the community, which is headed by an abbot. During the Middle Ages the monasteries became great centres of learning and they preserved many ancient manuscripts.

Saints and martyrs

Perhaps the most popular saint of all is St Francis (*c*.1181– 1226CE), who was born into a rich Italian family but renounced his wealth when he felt God calling him to a life of service. One night while he was praying, an angel is said to have appeared to him and given him the *stigmata* – wounds to his hands, feet and side in imitation of Christ's wounds on the cross.

Over the years many men and women have been persecuted for their faith and been martyred for it. The first Christian martyr was St Stephen, who was charged with blasphemy (speaking disrespectfully about God) by the Jewish authorities and stoned to death in Jerusalem in about 35CE. Many martyrs became holy figures venerated by the Church. St Catherine of Alexandria was a 4th-century saint and martyr who opposed Roman persecution and was strapped to a spiked wheel and tortured to death. The Catherine wheel has given its name to a firework that spins round when lit. The Roman Catholic Church uses a process known as 'canonization' to declare someone a saint and requires evidence of great devotion and some sort of miraculous event associated with their life. However, numerous men and women who have led saintly lives have not been officially declared saints.

Above *Religious men and women are not always confined to monasteries and convents. Here an African nun helps care for sick children at a medical mission.*

DIVISIONS IN CHRISTIANITY

Many Christians find it sad that the community that Jesus Christ founded as a unified family of believers is deeply divided. Divisions emerged shortly after Christ's death, when early Christians disagreed over the exact detail of his teaching and how it should be put into practice. The first major split or schism was in 1054CE, when the Church divided into two branches – eastern and western.

The eastern or Orthodox tradition

This grew out of the Byzantine Empire (the eastern part of the Roman Empire) of which Constantinople became the capital in 476CE. Its influence spread to Greece, central Europe and Russia, and the most important groups today are the Russian, Greek, Armenian, Serbian and Romanian Orthodox Churches that put great emphasis on tradition.

Above The traditions of the eastern Orthodox Church have remained unchanged for centuries.

The western or Roman Catholic tradition

The western tradition produced a Church based on the authority of the Bishop of Rome, who is in direct succession to the apostle Simon (later called Peter). The Pope is held to be infallible – in other words, his opinion on theological matters cannot be wrong and must be followed by Roman Catholics everywhere. The refusal by the Orthodox Church to accept papal authority was one of the reasons for the Great Schism. Roman Catholics are the largest group of Christians today, with around 890 million adherents. Outside Europe, South America has most Roman Catholics.

Below Barbara Harris was the first female bishop of the Episcopal Church of the United States. The role of women in the ordained ministry of the Christian Church is a source of deep theological division.

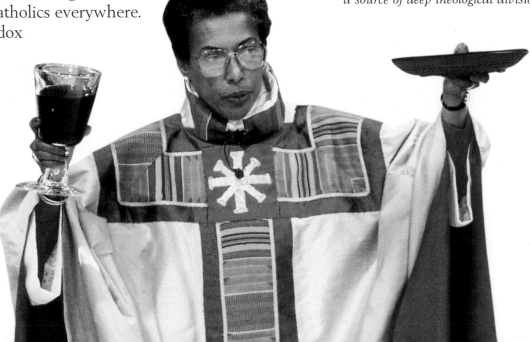

Above Evangelical or Charismatic worship is informal and spontaneous. These people are praying at a religious service at Newport Beach, California.

Below Pope John Paul II gives First Communion to Roman Catholic children in Trondheim, Norway. The Pope is the head of the Roman Catholic Church.

The Protestants

The Reformation began in the 14th century when people like Jan Hus, a preacher in Prague, attacked the Roman Catholic Church for its excessive wealth and its departure from the simple teaching of Christ. But most people date the Reformation from 1517, when the German theologian Martin Luther nailed 95 criticisms ('theses') of the Church to the door of the cathedral in Wittenberg. He argued that people did not need priests and the pope to mediate between themselves and God. He stressed a personal relationship with Christ and a close study of the Bible as a way towards salvation. His followers – who protested – became known as Protestants.

Many denominations

Despite internal tensions the Roman Catholic Church continues to be a unified body, but Protestantism has fragmented into many different denominations – Anglicanism, Lutheranism, Methodism, Presbyterianism and many others that share the core beliefs about Jesus Christ and his ministry but worship in different ways. A modern phenomenon in the West is the so-called House Church Movement, which has abandoned the traditional institutions of the church and worships in an informal style. Members tend to belong to the Evangelical or Charismatic wing of Christianity, that is to say, they put great emphasis on the gifts of the spirit and on a personal encounter with Jesus Christ. There are some theological disagreements between the liberal wing of the Church and those Evangelicals who interpret the Bible in a more literal way, but all Christians are trying to wrestle with the challenges contained in the Gospel and to make the faith a living reality in their lives.

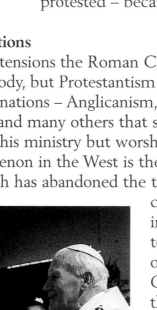

ISLAM: AN INTRODUCTION

Islam, which is translated as 'submission to God', is the religion practised by Muslims, who number around a thousand million worldwide. It is based on the teaching of the Prophet Muhammad, who is believed to have received the revealed word of Allah (God) some 1,400 years ago, in what is now Saudi Arabia.

The final revelation
Muslims believe that aspects of the divine message to humanity were also revealed to the prophets of the past (including Moses and Jesus), but that Muhammad was the last of the prophets to bring Allah's final message to the world. The message is contained in the Koran, Islam's holy book, which cannot be changed or added to. Such is the reverence for Muhammad that whenever the faithful speak his name they respectfully say after it, "peace be upon him".

It is said that the message of Allah was revealed to Muhammad by the chief angel Jibril, or Gabriel. Christians believe that Gabriel, who the Koran also records, appeared to the Virgin Mary to foretell Jesus' birth. The revelations of Jibril were not given all at once, but over a period of years. They were brought together in the Koran, the Muslim holy book. This is believed to contain a complete system of belief and practice binding on Muslims everywhere.

Above Muslims submit themselves to the will of God by prostrating themselves in worship. They can pray alone or, as here, with their fellow Muslims in a public display of devotion that is very impressive.

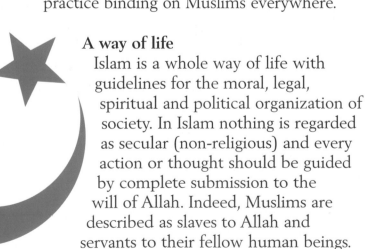

A way of life
Islam is a whole way of life with guidelines for the moral, legal, spiritual and political organization of society. In Islam nothing is regarded as secular (non-religious) and every action or thought should be guided by complete submission to the will of Allah. Indeed, Muslims are described as slaves to Allah and servants to their fellow human beings.

Left The hilal, or crescent moon and star, is the symbol of Islam. In the Koran it says that Allah created the stars to guide people to their destination. The moon is a reminder that the Islamic year is governed by the lunar calendar.

Above This 16th-century Persian engraving shows pupils studying the Holy Book at the feet of their teacher.

Below Children are expected to study the Koran and to be able to recite large parts of it by heart.

A revolutionary message

Islam emerged at a time when Judaism, Christianity and polytheism (worship of many gods) existed alongside each other on the Arabian peninsula. Many worshipped idols, so Muhammad's revolutionary message of the 'One Creator God' was upsetting and people rejected it. And yet, within 30 years, Islam became a powerful religion and later the basis of an influential Islamic empire. Islam teaches that Allah the Merciful will judge all our actions when we die. If we have done what is good and lawful (*halal*) we will be rewarded with eternity in heaven; if we have done what is not permitted (*haram*) we will go to hell. Islam is sometimes misunderstood in the West and the term 'Muslim fundamentalist' is frequently used as an insult. It is also misleading – all Muslims take their faith very seriously, so it is natural for them to follow fundamental principles. An increasingly secular West sometimes finds such devotion hard to understand.

THE DEVELOPMENT OF ISLAM

Islam developed first in Mecca, the birthplace of the Prophet Muhammad, and later in Medina. Mecca was situated on one of the principal trade routes in the Middle East, a location that may have helped Islam to be 'exported' throughout the world.

Early beginnings

At first Islam was no more than a localized sect of a few believers led by a man who believed Allah was revealing His message to him. This belief brought Muhammad and his followers into conflict with the merchants of Mecca, who did not want an important (and profitable) place of pilgrimage for Arab pagan beliefs threatened by the message that there was only One God. Muhammad and his followers were persecuted and eventually forced to leave. They moved north to Yathrib (later named Medina) in a migration that became known as the *hijra*. It marks the beginning of Islam as an organized religion.

Above The influence of local architectural styles can be seen in this mosque in Mali, west Africa. The mosque is made of mud.

Medina

At Medina, the Prophet Muhammad continued to receive divine revelations, among them rules of law that he applied to the growing community of Muslim believers. By now Mecca was hostile to Medina and launched a series of unsuccessful raids on the city. Muhammad was a skilled military leader who not only resisted attack but led an armed force of his own on Mecca in 630CE to cleanse the city of its pagan worship.

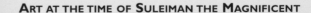

ART AT THE TIME OF SULEIMAN THE MAGNIFICENT

In the reign of the Ottoman Sultan, Suleiman the Magnificent (1520–1566CE), Islamic art and science flourished. At its height, the Ottoman Empire was one of the most influential in world history. The empire lasted until the end of World War I. Its capital, Constantinople (now Istanbul), was the centre of Islamic thought and produced a culture that embraced everything from ceramics and calligraphy, to architecture and astronomy. This mosque lamp of the period is characteristically ornate and comes from one of the numerous mosques that were constructed during Suleiman the Magnificent's reign.

Above This battle scene is from the 16th-century Book of Conquests by Suleiman. All Muslims are expected to defend Islam against outside threat by means of Jihad, or holy war. This also refers to a person's inner struggle against sin and temptation.

Muhammad's army met little resistance and he was able to take Mecca virtually without bloodshed. Many people who were initially hostile to Islam now embraced it and became Muslims themselves. One of the Prophet Muhammad's first tasks was to cleanse the Ka'ba (*see* page 134), of its idols and to return it to its original purity as a focal-point for worship of the One God. To this day it remains Islam's holiest site.

Expansion

When the Prophet died in 632CE there was disagreement over who should succeed him – a disagreement that later resulted in the division between the Sunni and Shi'a branches of Islam. Muhammad's successor was his father-in-law, Abu Bakr, who became the caliph (*khalifa*), or head of state. Under the first four caliphs, Islam expanded at a colossal rate into present-day Egypt, Syria, Iraq and Iran.

After the caliphs the Umayyad dynasty (661–750CE) took the faith west as far as Spain and Morocco and east as far as India. Their successors, the Abbasids (750–1258CE), made Baghdad (in present-day Iraq) their capital and extended their territory still further into central Asia. In 1258, the Mongols took control of Baghdad and became Muslims themselves. In 1453, Constantinople (the Christian capital of the Byzantine Empire) fell to the Ottoman Turks and was eventually renamed Istanbul. Islam experienced another period of renewal in 1979, when the Iranian Revolution deposed the ruling monarch, the Shah of Iran, and introduced an Islamic state under the leadership of Ayatollah Khomeini.

THE LIFE OF THE PROPHET

Muhammad was born 570CE in the Arabian city of Mecca and was orphaned at the age of six. He was raised first by his grandfather, then by an uncle.

Early life

When Muhammad was a young man he went to work for a rich widow, Khadijah, whose camels and caravans he looked after. The city of Mecca was home to the Ka'ba, the 'sacred house' said to have been built by Abraham and his son Ishmael. In Muhammad's time it was filled with pagan idols worshipped by Arabian tribes who visited Mecca on pilgrimage. The merchants were happy with this arrangement because the pilgrims were a source of income. When he was 25, Muhammad married Khadijah and had several children by her. He became rich and highly respected in the city, but was uneasy with the pagan worship around him and sought solitude in the deserts and mountains.

Above The Dome of the Rock in Jerusalem houses the rock from which it is said that Muhammad ascended into Heaven.

The message from God

Aged 40, Muhammad was meditating in a cave outside Mecca when the Angel Jibril appeared. Jibril ordered Muhammad to read but when he replied that he could not, the Angel squeezed him tightly and insisted. "Read," he said, "read in the name of your Lord who created you from a drop of blood." This was the first message that he received directly from Allah.

Left The Prophet's cave at Jebel Nur in present-day Saudi Arabia. Some Muslims believe this is where Adam, the first man created by Allah, appeared on Earth.

Above This print shows a caravan of pilgrims on the road to Mecca. In the past Muslims from all over the world travelled by foot, on horseback or camel. The journey could take years, so the pilgrims met many people along the way. Nowadays modern air travel means that Mecca is only hours away.

> "Be steadfast in prayer. Practise regular charity and bow down your heads with those who bow down in worship."
>
> The Koran 2:43

The Night Journey

In about the tenth year of his ministry, Muhammad is said to have undergone a miraculous experience. In what has come to be called the Night Journey, he is said to have been taken up into the sky in the company of the angels. From Mecca he was taken to Jerusalem, where he prayed with the earlier prophets including Abraham, Moses and Jesus. After this, from a rock now contained in the Dome of the Rock in Jerusalem, he is believed to have ascended to heaven into the presence of Allah Himself, who told him to institute prayers five times a day.

The message spreads

Forced out of Mecca by persecution, Muhammad became the ruler of Medina, which was the target of hostilities by the people of Mecca. When Muhammad took Mecca in 630CE, he behaved with such generosity and tolerance that many of his former enemies became Muslims themselves. Two years after he had cleansed the Ka'ba of its pagan worship and restored it to the one god, Muhammad gave his last sermon to the people and declared that his aim in life was complete – he had delivered the word of Allah, which would remain true for all time. At the age of 63, Muhammad died in Medina, where he was buried.

THE KORAN

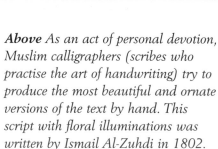

The Koran is the holy book of the Muslim world. The word means 'reading' and is taken from the instruction the Angel Jibril gave Muhammad (*see* page 134), that he should read the word of God.

Learning by heart

Because the revelation was in Arabic, Muslims have always studied the Koran in its original language. Very often, for boys and girls starting out on study, this means reciting the words while not fully understanding what they mean. However, since the words are believed to be the actual words of Allah, merely reciting them is seen as an act of worship in itself. Students are encouraged to learn as much of the Koran as they can by heart and in 1998 a six-year-old Muslim girl in South Africa became the youngest girl ever to have memorized the whole text in Arabic – 114 *suras* (chapters) in all, divided into verses.

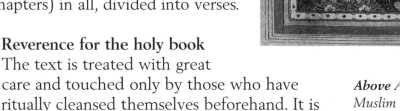

Reverence for the holy book

The text is treated with great care and touched only by those who have ritually cleansed themselves beforehand. It is often wrapped in ornate cloth and kept in a special place in the home or mosque. Unlike the Ten Commandments, the Koran was not handed over at one single event in history, but over a period of 23 years. As a result it contains different styles of writing that deal with all aspects of life. There are instructions on how to pray, how to organize society and how to apply the law. It lists rules for the structure of family life, the duties of individuals to behave well, and penalties for sinners on Judgement Day. Above all, it stresses the 'Oneness' of Allah and the need to obey Him.

Above As an act of personal devotion, Muslim calligraphers (scribes who practise the art of handwriting) try to produce the most beautiful and ornate versions of the text by hand. This script with floral illuminations was written by Ismail Al-Zuhdi in 1802.

Left This boy is studying the Koran in Arabic at the Islamic School in London. In the Indian and Pakistani tradition, pupils sit round the edge of the schoolroom, not in rows behind each other. This is because it is considered disrespectful to have one's back to the Holy Book.

Other sources of guidance

Because Muhammad is believed to have led an exemplary life, his actions and sayings are considered to be of importance to Muslims. Stories of the Prophet's life are taken as practical examples of how devout Muslims should try to lead their own lives. Consequently, the traditional customs and practices of the Prophet (the *Sunna*) and his words and sayings (the *Haddith*) are consulted alongside the Koran and, with it, provide the faithful with a complete guide book to a godly life.

Although there are divisions within Islam and scholars from different traditions around the world may interpret the text in different ways, all Muslims accept the ultimate authority of the Koran over their lives and try to live by its rules.

> "This is the Book. In it is guidance sure, without doubt to those who fear God."
>
> The Koran 2:2

Below Some Muslims believe that the original version of the Koran has existed since the beginning of time on tablets stored in heaven. The text is venerated as the complete revelation of Allah's holy word.

MECCA AND THE FIVE PILLARS OF ISLAM

Mecca, the birthplace of the Prophet Muhammad, is a holy city and a place of pilgrimage for over two million Muslims every year. The pilgrimage, which all healthy Muslim men and women are expected to make at least once in a lifetime, is known as the *Hajj* and is the fifth of the 'Pillars of Islam'.

The *shahada*

Just as the pillars in a mosque support the building that rises above them, so the Pillars of Islam support the beliefs and practices of the Islamic faith. The first pillar is the statement of faith – the *shahada*.

Below At the centre of the holy city of Mecca is the Ka'ba, a cube-shaped shrine covered in black and gold velvet. When Muslim pilgrims visit the Ka'ba, they walk round it seven times in an anti-clockwise direction reciting prayers to Allah.

Left Regular prayer is central to Islamic practice. The women and children worship apart from the men.

It says, "There is no god but Allah and Muhammad is the Messenger of Allah". In reciting these words of faith, devout Muslims proclaim their belief in one God and their conviction that God's teaching has been revealed to Muhammad. This simple statement is the basis of all Muslim belief. It is the first thing whispered into a child's ear when he or she is born, and the last thing a Muslim hopes to utter at the moment of death.

Salat and zakat

The second pillar, *salat*, is daily worship – the prayers that are recited five times a day, at dawn, midday, afternoon, evening and night. Muslims stop what they are doing to bow down in worship in the direction of Mecca. The third pillar is *zakat*, or charitable giving. This has two functions. The first is to copy the generosity that Allah shows towards his people, and the second is to show kindness in a practical way to those less well off.

> **"I bear witness that there is no God but Allah and I bear witness that Muhammad is the messenger of Allah."**
>
> Words from the *shahada*

Sawm

The fourth pillar is fasting or *sawm*, which involves going without food and drink during daylight hours throughout the holy month

of Ramadan. For people with jobs, and children who have school to attend, total abstinence is not easy, but it does bring spiritual reward. The end of Ramadan is celebrated with the festival of Eid ul-Fitr when presents are exchanged.

Left The religious duties of which the Five Pillars are the core are taught to Muslims such as this Algerian girl at an early age.

ISLAMIC LAW AND SCIENCE

The system of Islamic law known as *Shari'a* comes from the Arabic word describing a track leading camels to a watering-hole – a description implying a pathway that, if followed by humanity, will lead to Allah.

Sources of the law
The Koran and the *Sunna* (customs and practices of the Prophet) are the two principal sources of the law in Islam. There are five categories of action: what Allah has decreed, what Allah has forbidden, what Allah has recommended but not insisted on, what Allah has disapproved of but not expressly forbidden and what Allah has remained silent about. An example of these distinctions is contained in Islam's attitude to alcohol and tobacco. The consumption of alcohol – an intoxicant – is definitely forbidden, but tobacco is different. Some scholars have argued that it is not covered in the Koran, although they suspect it is a grey area that, while not expressly forbidden, is disapproved of. As a result Muslims may smoke pipes or cigarettes and still be within the law.

Above Islamic law deals with all aspects of family life. A man may have more than one wife, provided he can look after them equally – an arrangement that is, however, increasingly rare in the West.

Interpreting the law
Shari'a deals with every aspect of human society including family life, property, crime, punishment, business and morality. In practice it has been supplemented with legislation adapted to suit the needs of different communities. Scholars constantly interpret the law and their findings also become a basis for law-making. Experts able to rule on points of law are known as *muftis*. Shi'a Muslims also accept the rulings of their highest religious leaders, the ayatollahs. Interpretation of Islamic law may vary, but its fundamentals will always apply.

Right Young women working in the laboratory in Egypt continue the centuries-old tradition of scholarship and science.

Above This painting shows astronomers at work in the 16th-century observatory in Istanbul. Globes, maps, astrolabes, telescopes and compasses have all been refined by Muslim scientists.

"It is God who sends the winds and they raise the clouds. Then does He spread them in the sky as He wills."

The Koran 30:48

Muslim scholarship

Throughout the Dark Ages of Europe (c.500–1100CE) the flame of scholarship was kept alive by writers, philosophers and mathematicians from the Islamic world, who translated many of the classical texts of ancient Greece into Arabic. The western system of numerals is of Arabic origin. By superseding Roman numerals, they made modern mathematics possible. Muslim mathematicians also gave the world algebra.

Astronomical exploration

Islamic scientists founded observatories from which they plotted the positions of the stars. They used and refined a special instrument known as an astrolabe, which enabled them to carry out a scientific function (measuring the angle of the stars and plotting distances and directions on the ground) and a religious function (establishing the direction of Mecca – the *qibla* – for their daily prayers). Astrolabes were important tools for navigation and map-making, and opened up the way for even more scientific discoveries. Islam, which has produced eminent philosophers, doctors and scientists, encourages scholarship, but it also teaches that Allah alone is the source of all knowledge and all creation.

WORSHIP AND FESTIVALS

Muslims believe that humans were created to worship God and the purpose of life itself is total submission to His will. *Salat*, the set prayers that are recited five times a day in the direction of Mecca, give a structure to the day. Muslims will often have a special prayer rug, or *sajjada*, for use in the home or when they are travelling. This allows them to create a ritually pure and holy space from which to direct their thoughts to Allah. In the home and in the mosque shoes are removed as a sign of reverence.

Above Five times a day Muslims stop whatever they are doing, face the direction of Mecca and prostrate themselves in prayer.

The festival year

Just as prayers punctuate the day, so do festivals punctuate the Islamic year, which has 12 lunar months, or 354 days. In some Islamic traditions the calendar begins with the celebration of the *hijra*, the Prophet's migration from Mecca to Medina in 622CE. This is followed two months later by a festival marking his birthday in 570CE.

The ninth month of Ramadan is the most significant of the year and it is marked by a complete abstinence from food and drink during the hours of daylight. It is believed that the Prophet received Allah's first revelation during Ramadan and as a result it is kept holy. Fasting is a physical and spiritual discipline designed to focus attention on Allah in a concentrated way and it is a duty that every fit and healthy adult is expected to perform. Children are not expected to fast, but many do so in imitation of their parents' devotion to Allah.

Left These children have a homemade Eid card. The end of Ramadan is associated with blessings and joy, and people often exchange presents.

Above Ramadan ends with the joyful festival of Eid ul-Fitr, when families and friends break their month-long fast.

"People, adore your Guardian–Lord who created you."

The Koran 2:21

Daily routine

In many households the day begins before dawn with prayers and a reading from the Koran. People then set off for work, school or college knowing that they will not be able to eat or drink anything until the Sun has set. Attendance at the mosque increases during Ramadan, particularly towards the end of the month when people gather to commemorate *Lailat al-Qadr*, the Night of Power, when it is believed Allah first revealed His holy law to the Prophet Muhammad. Muslims try to stay awake all night and may remain in the mosque praying or reciting from the Koran. The fast concentrates mind, body and spirit on Allah and demonstrates that it is important to resist temptation. It is also thought to be a way for the rich to experience the hardship of the poor.

Fasting for a feast

Ramadan ends as soon as the new Moon is sighted – in some Muslim countries this is signalled by the sound of a canon. The fasting stops and Muslims prepare for the joyful festival of Eid ul-Fitr, when they sit down to enjoy their first meal during daylight for a month. Richer families are expected to give food to the poor so that everyone can mark the day happily. Often presents are exchanged, symbolizing the blessings and happiness that await all those who follow Allah's will.

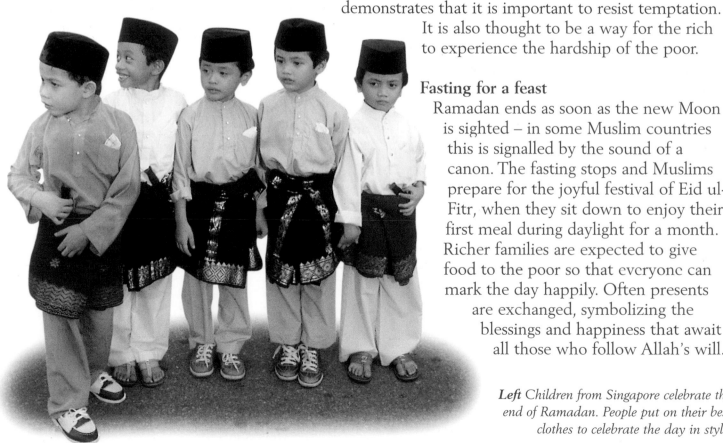

Left Children from Singapore celebrate the end of Ramadan. People put on their best clothes to celebrate the day in style.

THE MOSQUE

The word 'mosque' comes from an Arabic word that means 'place of prostration'. It is the house of prayer where Muslims gather together to worship Allah. There are many different styles of mosque, and they reflect the traditional architecture of the countries in which they are found. However, all of them share common design features.

Pointers to Allah

Perhaps the most distinctive element of a mosque is its minaret, the tall, slender tower designed to be seen from a distance as a reminder of Allah's presence. As one's gaze is taken up the minaret to the top, one is symbolically looking up towards heaven, where Allah is supreme. Similarly, the dome of the mosque symbolizes the roof of the sky where Allah reigns in splendour and majesty.

The harmony of creation

Although the mosque will often be richly decorated, the decorations are always abstract and geometrical, symbolizing divine harmony. Because Muslims are anxious to avoid the sin of idolatry (worshipping anything other than the One God), there are never any pictures of people or animals that might accidentally distract the worshipper from Allah alone.

House of prayer

The mosque is usually full at midday on Friday, which is an important day for communal worship. Unlike Judaism and Christianity, Islam has no concept of the Sabbath. As Allah never stops working, Muslims believe that they should not stop working either.

Left Traditionally the muezzin *(or proclaimer) calls the faithful to prayer from the minaret or tower of the mosque. In most Islamic countries the task is now carried out electronically through a loudspeaker system.*

The *mihrab* is a niche in the wall that marks the direction of Mecca.

The *minbar* is a pulpit from which the *imam* delivers his sermon on Fridays.

The minarets have balconies from which the call to prayer is given by the *muezzin*.

Left The Blue Mosque in Istanbul is one of the most beautiful religious buildings in the world. It was built between 1609 and 1616CE on the orders of Sultan Ahmet I.

Above Men congregate for prayer at the Prophet's Mosque in Medina, Saudi Arabia. They kneel on carpets and face Mecca.

Once they have said Friday prayers, they resume their working day. Prayer is led by a religious leader (*imam*) or by a preacher (*khatib*). When praying, Muslims always face Mecca – the direction is indicated by an empty niche or alcove known as the *mihrab*. Because prayer involves ritual movements of standing, kneeling and bowing, the space in the main prayer hall has no seating of any kind. Instead carpets cover the floor, marking it out as holy ground. Although some mosques have a separate space for women to worship, mosque prayer is usually an all-male activity. Worshippers leave their shoes at the door and proceed to a small room – usually a communal space with low seats in front of individual taps – where they rinse their hands, face, nostrils, mouth, arms and feet in ritual purification.

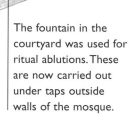

The fountain in the courtyard was used for ritual ablutions. These are now carried out under taps outside walls of the mosque.

Equality in the sight of Allah

In the prayer hall the worshippers line up together – young, old, rich and poor occupying the same space to show that all are equal in the sight of Allah. Next to the *mihrab* is the *minbar*, resembling a small staircase, from which the preacher delivers his sermon, or *khutba*. Mosque worship is based on the word of Allah so there is no singing or music of any kind. Muslims believe that corporate worship is more pleasing to Allah than individual prayer, so they make a special effort to attend.

DIVISION AND DIVERSITY

The Koran describes Muhammad as 'the Seal of the Prophets', that is to say, with him the line of the prophets (beginning with Adam and continuing through Abraham, Moses and Jesus) has been sealed for all time. Muhammad is the last and no other will follow him.

After the Prophet

Problems arose after the Prophet's death when there was disagreement about who should lead the Muslim community. Two branches, Sunni and Shi'a, emerged. The Sunnis took their name from the *Sunna*, or traditions of the Prophet. They argued that as no one could ever equal Muhammad in wisdom and goodness, his chosen successor had to be the person judged most suitable by the community. The Prophet's first successor was Abu Bakr, who became the first of the four caliphs who ruled the (as yet) undivided *umma*, or community of believers.

Above From 1979–1989 the influence of Ayatollah Khomeini was important in defining the character of Shi'a Islam. The revolution he inspired in Iran, and his insistence on a particular type of Islamic purity, brought him into direct conflict with countries in the West.

The decisive split

The group who were eventually to become the Shi'as were unhappy with this arrangement and argued that only Muhammad's nearest relative, his cousin and son-in-law Ali, was fit to follow in the Prophet's footsteps. Becoming known as the 'followers of the party of Ali' or 'shi'at Ali' (Shi'a for short), they believed that Ali had inherited some of the qualities and authority of their founder, qualities that made him especially suitable to become their religious leader, or *imam*. The decisive split between Sunnis and Shi'as came in 680CE, when Ali's son Hussain was killed by Muslim rivals at the Battle of Karbala. His tomb in what is now southern Iraq is still regarded as one of the holiest shrines in the Shi'a Islamic world.

Right These Chinese children reciting parts of the Koran in Arabic show how far Islam has travelled from its beginnings on the Arabian Peninsula.

Above Islamic dress should be modest at all times, but different countries interpret modesty differently. These Afghanistan women wear a very conservative style of dress that leaves only the eyes visible, and these are also sometimes covered by a veil.

Shi'as and Sunnis

Shiism itself soon divided, this time into three groups. The majority Imami, or Twelver, group, found mostly in Iran, Iraq and Lebanon, believed in 12 principal *imams*, the twelfth of whom is said to have disappeared, but will return at the end of time. The Ismailis, or Severner, group supported a man named Ismail as the seventh *Imam* in his claim to be the head of Shiism. The Ziadis, the third group, are found mostly in Yemen. Sunni Muslims account for some 90 per cent of the world's Islamic population. A principal centre of Sunni Islam is Saudi Arabia, which is also guardian of the most important religious shrine in Mecca. Shi'a Muslims, most of whom live in Iran, account for the remaining 10 per cent.

> **"When you recite the Koran, seek refuge in God from accursed Satan."**
>
> The Koran 16:98

147

THE WAY OF THE SUFI

T he Sufis are not a separate branch of Islam. They can be drawn from both the Sunni and Shi'a groups and are defined by their mystical approach to the faith. Taking their name from the *suf* – the simple woollen robe they used to wear (*suf* means 'wool') – they search for a closer, personal relationship with Allah. Sufism was influenced by the ascetic practices (giving up material possessions) of Christian monks and hermits. Like them, Sufis turned their back on the world and took vows of poverty.

The mystical tradition

During a service known as a *dhikr*, Sufis use singing, dance and drumming to focus all their attention on Allah. In this state of heightened concentration on the divine presence, they hope to forget themselves and the everyday world completely so that their soul can be free to unite with Allah Himself. The Sufi tradition produced the most famous female mystic in Islam's history: Rabi'a al-Adawiyya (721–801CE) was a slave girl who devoted her life entirely to Allah.

Closer communion with God

In the 12th century CE, a number of Sufi orders or brotherhoods (*tariqas*) sprang up and were based in enclosed communities set aside for study and prayer. Perhaps the best known of the Sufi groups that the *tariqas* produced are the Dervishes, whose name comes from the Turkish and Persian words meaning 'beggar'. They, too, took vows of poverty and devoted their lives to union with Allah. Following the guidance of a religious teacher (a *shaykh* or *pir*), they practise rituals that induce an almost hypnotic or trance-like state in which they hope to come into a closer union with Allah.

Left This woman uses prayer beads to aid her devotion. They are a physical way of helping the mind to focus on Allah.

Above Whirling Dervishes of the Turkish Sufi sect spin round to induce a trance-like state which, it is believed, brings them into a closer relationship with Allah.

The Whirling Dervishes

Unlike other Muslim groups, the Sufis use ritual music in their devotions. The group popularly called the Whirling Dervishes rotate round and round to the accompaniment of a repetitive beat, seeking a higher level of consciousness that they hope will ultimately bring them into direct contact with Allah. The whirling is said to imitate the rotation of the planets round the Sun and that of the whole of creation round Allah. For some Muslims, music is considered ungodly because it can lead to temptation, but for Sufis it is often used as an actual aid to devotion. Sufi mysticism appeals as much to the heart as to the head, and at its centre is the simple but all-consuming love of Allah.

MODERN DAY BELIEFS

Religious belief is not fixed. It is developing constantly as men and women of every generation seek new answers to some of life's old questions. Dissatisfied with the religions they see around them, some may invent new religious movements, while others will look to existing religions, borrow elements from them, and add new ones of their own.

The Church of Jesus Christ of Latter-day Saints

Members of this church are known as Mormons. This name derives from one of their central scriptures, the *Book of Mormon*, which their founder, Joseph Smith (1805–1844), claimed to have translated under divine guidance. It is believed to be another Testament to be studied alongside the Old and New Testaments of the Bible.

Mormons believe that Jesus Christ visited what is now called America and that their Church is a restoration on Earth of Christ's Church. They believe Jesus will come again and institute a thousand-year reign, after which Satan and the forces of evil will be defeated. This doctrine is known as millenarianism, and is shared by other groups influenced by mainstream Christianity. With more than 10 million members worldwide the Church is growing fast. It has no paid clergy, but young men and women are expected to complete a period of missionary service abroad to spread the gospel.

Mormons lead a disciplined life, avoiding intoxicants such as alcohol or tobacco, and they have a strong self-help philosophy.

Above *The Church of Jesus Christ of Latter-day Saints (Mormons) re-enact the Long March of 1847, when Mormon pioneers trekked across the plains of America from winter quarters to the valley of the Great Salt Lake.*

Left *Although some modern-day Druids claim to be in a tradition stretching back to Celtic Druids, the modern order was founded only some 300 years ago. Their rituals centre on the elements of air, fire and water, and on a reverence for the earth.*

Other Christian-influenced groups

Seventh Day Adventists also have a millenarian philosophy and believe that the second coming of Christ is not far off. They observe Saturday as the sabbath, or day of rest.

Jehovah's Witnesses spread their message through door-to-door evangelism, but reject much of traditional Christian doctrine. For example, they deny the idea of the Trinity (God as Father, Son and Holy Spirit) and they forbid their members to have blood transfusions.

Baha'i

The Baha'i faith was originally an offshoot of Islam and was founded by Mirza Husayn Ali Nuri in 1863CE. At first he had been a follower of a man known as 'the Bab', who preached that Muhammad was not the last of the prophets, but that a messenger of God was still to come. Nuri took the name Baha'u'lla (Glory of God) and taught that all religions are basically one and that people should strive for world peace and harmony between the world's faiths.

Hare Krishna

One of the most distinctive of the Hindu-inspired groups is the Hare Krishna movement. Devotees put the god Krishna at the centre of their worship and they sing a *mantra* (a short repetitive phrase) based on his name. Yoga, meditation and daily readings from their scriptures are part of their devotions.

Right The International Society for Krishna Consciousness (ISKON) was founded in 1966. Hare Krishna devotees worship the Hindu god Krishna.

151

Finding a way

In every generation there are those whose spiritual longings are not satisfied by existing religions and who decide to establish religious movements of their own. In our own age, countless new beliefs have emerged. Only time will tell whether they will flourish or wither away.

Rastafarians

Rastafarianism, which is practised largely in Jamaica and the Caribbean, has at its heart devotion to the late Emperor Haile Selassie, born Tafari Makonnen, of Ethiopia (1892–1975). Its followers consider him (also known as Prince, or 'Ras' Tafari) a saviour who will lead the black people to their sacred homeland of Africa and deliver them from what they see as the oppression of the white people.

Followers of Rastafarianism look to the Hebrew Bible to define their identity and believe that they are the descendants of the twelve tribes of Israel (*see* page 88). In particular, they believe that they are fulfilling Psalm 68, which tells of God's liberation of the oppressed. Using the name contained in verse 4 of that psalm, they refer to God as 'Jah'. Perhaps the most famous Rasta of modern times was the singer Bob Marley (1945–1981) who, through his music, brought the culture of Rastafarianism to a mass audience.

The New Age Movement

This term is used to describe a number of different groups which, while they have no creeds or structured belief system, have certain elements in common. Typically, new age believers in the West borrow from Eastern religions and focus particularly on healing and the environment.

Above *Members of the Unification Church (the 'Moonies') take part in a mass wedding. The movement was founded in Korea in 1954 by the Reverend Sun Myung Moon. His controversial teachings blend elements of Christianity and Taoism.*

Left *Although in the Christian tradition, tele-evangelism has developed a character of its own by reinterpreting an old message in a new way and using modern mass communication to spread the Gospel message.*

Many believe that the Earth contains unseen energies that can be channelled to promote good health and a sense of well-being. These energies are believed to be found in places (prehistoric sites associated with worship, myth, magic or legend), or things (crystals, perfumes or colours). The movement also includes modern pagan worshippers who look to the Earth as a source of fertility and power.

"There is only one religion, though there are a hundred versions of it."

George Bernard Shaw

Good or bad

Some of those people who feel the need to form a new religion are well-meaning with a real concern to share what they see as the truth of existence. But some are motivated by power or money and want to found a religion only to control other people's lives. As a result, alongside those new religious movements which are harmless and beneficial, there are some dangerous cults which demand absolute obedience and which, in extreme instances, have forced their members to harm themselves. The intentions of such new religions will become clear over time.

Throughout history, people have often had to suffer for their beliefs – sometimes being made fun of, being punished, or even being killed. People who have clung onto their beliefs whatever the price have shown how powerful religions can be. Having embarked on the great adventure of faith, they continue to trust that, though the cost may be great, the reward will be greater still.

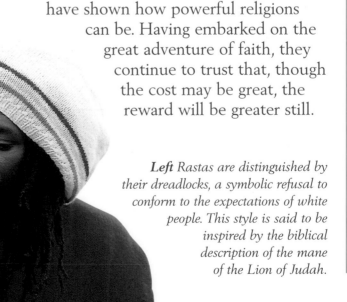

Left Rastas are distinguished by their dreadlocks, a symbolic refusal to conform to the expectations of white people. This style is said to be inspired by the biblical description of the mane of the Lion of Judah.

Glossary

Adi Granth The Sikh holy book which is treated as if it were a revered teacher, hence its other name, the *Guru Granth Sahib*.

Ahimsa In Hindu, Buddhist, and Jain belief, the respect for all living things and principle of non-violence.

Ahura Mazda The creator and god of Zoroastrianism.

Ancestor worship In Chinese and Shinto belief and in native religions, the practice of venerating dead relatives.

Ascetic A person who practises extreme self-discipline in order to develop spiritually.

Avatar In Hinduism one of ten earthly manifestations of the creator god, Vishnu.

Baptism The Christian rite involving the ceremonial use of water and signifying formal admission to the Church.

Conversion A change in one's religious direction through adoption of a new belief.

Covenant A bargain or agreement, especially that between God and the Israelites.

Creed An agreed set of beliefs.

Dharma In Hinduism, the eternal law of the universe. In Buddhism, the teachings of the Buddha.

Dreamtime In the Aboriginal tradition, the period of creation when ancestral beings roamed the Earth and formed the landscape.

Druids Ancient Celtic priests.

Eucharist Also known as Holy Communion, eucharist is the Christian sacrament commemorating with bread and wine Jesus Christ's last meal with his disciples before his death and resurrection.

Fasting Abstaining from food as part of a spiritual discipline.

Five Pillars of Islam The principal duties every Muslim must carry out: the profession of faith in the one god, daily prayer, charitable giving, fasting during the month of Ramadan, pilgrimage to Mecca.

Gospels The first four books of the New Testament of the Bible that describe the life and teachings of Jesus Christ.

Guru In Hinduism, a spiritual teacher, and in Sikhism one of the ten early leaders of the faith.

Hadith In Islam, the collection of sayings and traditions of the Prophet Muhammad.

Halakah Jewish religious law.

Heaven In many religious traditions, the home of God or the gods and the place to which the good will go when they die.

Hell A place of eternal torment reserved for the wicked.

Incarnation The Christian doctrine stating that God took human form in the person of Jesus Christ.

Jihad A holy war in defence of Islam and the personal struggle within oneself to lead a godly life.

Kami In Shinto, unseen spirits which live in the natural landscape.

Karma In Hinduism and Buddhism, the eternal law of cause and effect. In Jainism, the invisible matter which attaches itself to the soul and prevents it from progressing.

Khalsa The community of pure, fully initiated Sikhs.

Lent The 40-day period of spiritual discipline preceding the Christian festival of Easter.

Lama A spiritual teacher within Tibetan Buddhism.

Libation The pouring out of a drink in honour of a god.

Mantra In Buddhism and Hinduism, a word or syllable repeated as part of meditation and believed to possess a spiritual power of its own.

Messiah In Judaism, the deliverer of the Jewish people as foretold in the Hebrew Bible. In the Christian tradition, Jesus Christ himself, whom Christians believe to be the Saviour of humankind.

Moksha In the Hindu and Jain traditions, release from the ongoing cycle of birth, death and rebirth.

Monasticism The religious tradition of withdrawing from the world to devote oneself to prayer and meditation.

Monotheism The doctrine that there is only one God.

New Age A loose collection of religious movements dating from the 1960s, mixing Eastern and Western spiritual traditions and focusing on the healing energies of the natural world.

Night Journey The Prophet Muhammad's supernatural journey across the sky from Mecca to Jerusalem from where he ascended into heaven and into the presence of Allah.

Nirvana In Buddhism, the release from all suffering and all desire into a state of perfect spiritual enlightenment.

Passover The Jewish festival commemorating the exodus of the Jews from Egypt.

Pilgrimage A journey to a sacred place.

Polytheism Belief in many gods.

Rabbi A religious teacher in the Jewish tradition.

Ragnarok In the Norse tradition, the end of the world and the beginning of a new heaven and a new Earth.

Ramadan The Islamic holy month during which the Prophet Muhammad received God's revelation.

Reincarnation Rebirth into a new body.

Repentance Turning away from wrongdoing, expressing sorrow for sins and resolving to do good.

Resurrection The return of Jesus Christ from the dead after his crucifixion.

Samsara In Hinduism, the continual cycle of birth, death and rebirth.

Shaman In traditional religion, a person believed to be capable of direct contact with the spirit world. Also known as a medicine man or witch-doctor.

Sharia Islamic religious law.

Sin The breaking of holy laws.

Torah The first five books of the Hebrew Bible containing God's laws.

Trickster gods In native religions, mischievous gods who change shape and appearance to show that the world can be a surprising and unpredictable place.

Trinity The Christian doctrine stating that in God there are three persons: God the Father, God the Son and God the Holy Spirit.

Umma The community of Muslim believers.

Voodoo A mixture of native African religion and Roman Catholicism practised on the Caribbean island of Haiti.

Yin and Yang Equal and opposite forces in Taoism. Yin: feminine, dark and passive. Yang: masculine, bright and active.

Yom Kippur The most solemn day of the Jewish calendar. Also known as the Day of Atonement, it is a time for repentance.

INDEX

ACKNOWLEDGEMENTS

3 Magnum Photos/Bruno Barbey.
4 Impact/Michael Mirecki, TL;
Michael Freeman, TR; Bridgeman
Art Library/Victoria & Albert
Museum, BL; Bridgeman Art
Library, BR. 5 Hutchison Library/
Liba Taylor, TL; Peter Sanders, MR;
Sonia Halliday, B. 6 Magnum Photos/
Steve McCurry, TR; Magnum
Photos/Abbas, BR. 7 Magnum
Photos/Jean Gaumy, TL; Trip, B.
8 Tim Slade, B. 9 Robert Harding,
TL. 10 Werner Forman Archive/
National Museum, Copenhagen, BL;
10-11 AKG, B; 11 Robert Harding,
TL; AKG/Erich Lessing, BR.
12 Hutchison Library/Jeremy A.
Horner, BL; 12-13 Michael Holford/
British Museum, T. 13 Bridgeman Art
Library/Oriental Museum, Durham
University, TR; Robert Harding, BL.
14 Roger Hutchins, TR; 14-15 Roger
Hutchins, B; 15 Trip/R. Cracknell,
TR. 16 Bridgeman Art Library/The
De Morgan Foundation, London,
TR; 16-17 Bridgeman Art Library/
Louvre, Paris. 17 Bridgeman Art
Library, TL; Michael Holford, MR.
18 E.T. Archive, TR; Collections/
Michael Diggin, BL. 19 Bridgeman
Art Library/Royal Library,
Copenhagen, TL. 20 Bridgeman Art
Library, TR; Ancient Art and
Architecture Collection, BM.
21 Ann and Bury Peerless, T;
Magnum Photos/Bruno Barbey, BL.
22 Bridgeman Art Library, TR;
Werner Forman, BR. 23 Trip, TR;
Impact/Michael Mirecki, BL.
24 Michael Holford, BL. 24-25 Trip/
T. Bognar, M. 25 Bridgeman Art
Library/National Library of
Australia, TR. 26 Bridgeman Art
Library/Corbally Stourton
Contemporary Art, London, TR;
Werner Forman, BL. 27 Bridgeman
Art Library, TL; Bridgeman Art
Library, BL. 28 Bridgeman Art
Library/Royal Ontario Museum, BM.
28-29 E.T. Archive. 29 Bridgeman
Art Library, BM. 30 Trip, TR; Still
Pictures, BL; 31 Trip/C. Treppe, TL;
Bridgeman Art Library, TR.
32-33 Peter Sanders, T; Robert
Harding, B. 33 Claire Pullinger, BR.
34 Bridgeman Art Library/National
Museum of India, BL. 34-35 Roger
Hutchins, M. 35 C.M. Dixon, TR.
36-37 Magnum Photos/Steve
McCurry. 37 Bridgeman Art Library,
TM; Bridgeman Art Library, BR.
38 Bridgeman Art Library, ML.
38-39 India Office Library.
40 Bridgeman Art Library/British
Library, TR; Frank Spooner, ML;
Bridgeman Art Library/Oriental
Museum, Durham University, BR.
41 Bridgeman Art Library/Victoria &

Albert Museum. 42 Hutchison
Library/Liba Taylor, TR; Tony Stone/
Mark Lewis, B. 43 Hutchison Library,
TL; Still Pictures/Sarvottam
Rajkoomar, BL. 44 British Library,
Oriental and India Office, TR; Robert
Harding, BL. 45 Hutchison Library/
K. Rodgers, TL. 46 Trip/H. Rogers,
BM. 46-47 Trip/Dinodia. 47 Trip/
Dinodia, TR. 48 Robert Harding,
ML; Hutchison Library/J. Horner,
BR. 49 Hutchison Library. 50 Trip/
H. Rogers, TR; Robert Harding, BL.
51 Bank of India. 52 Trip/H. Rogers,
TR; Robert Harding, BM. 53 Michael
Freeman, T; Magnum Photos/Raghu
Rai, BL. 54 Magnum Photos/Raghu
Rai, BL; 54-55 Michael Freeman.
55 Robert Harding/Jeremy Bright,
TR; Format/Judy Harrison, BR.
56 Format/Judy Harrison, BL.
56-57 Panos/Liba Taylor, T.
57 Michael Freeman, BR. 58 Michael
Freeman, B. 59 Michael Freeman,
TL; Bridgeman Art Library/
Christie's, BR. 60 Michael Freeman,
TM; Michael Freeman, MR.
61 Bridgeman Art Library/Oriental
Museum, Durham University.
62 Bridgeman Art Library/Osaka
Museum of Fine Arts, BL; E.T.
Archive/British Library, TR.
63 Sygma, T. 64 Trip/B. Vikander, BL.
64-65 Magnum Photos/Raghu Rai, T.
65 Magnum Photos/Ferdinando
Scianna, TR; Network/E. Grames/
Bildenberg, BL. 66 Michael Freeman,
TR; 66-67 Mitchell Beazley. 67 Michael
Freeman, TL; Michael Freeman, BR.
68 Michael Freeman, TR; *Fuji Above
the Lightning from the series
36 Views of Mount Fuji* by Hokusai/
Bridgeman Art Library/Fitzwilliam
Museum, BL. 69 E.T. Archive, T; Tim
Slade, BL. 70 Michael Freeman, TR;
Michael Freeman, B. 71 Trip/P.Rauter,
TL; Michael Freeman, BL; Network/
Gideon Mendel, MR. 72 E.T.
Archive, TR; Still Pictures, BL.
73 E.T. Archive/British Museum, TL;
Bridgeman Art Library/British
Museum, BR. 74 Bridgeman Art
Library/Bibliotheque Nationale, BL;
Bridgeman Art Library, TR. 75 E.T.
Archive/British Museum, TL.
76 Robert Harding, TR, Hutchison
Library/Ian Lloyd, BR. 77 Bridgeman
Art Library, T. 78 Bridgeman Art
Library, BL. 78-79 Hutchison
Library/John Hatt, T. 79 Bridgeman
Art Library/Oriental Museum,
Durham University, BR. 80 Magnum
Photos/Fred Mayer, BL.
80-81 Hutchison Library/Robert
Francis. 81 Magnum Photos/Bruno
Barbey, BR. 82 Robert Harding, TR;
Magnum Photos/Fred Mayer, BR.
83 Trip/A. Tovy. 84 Trip/A. Tovy,

BM; 84-85 Hutchison Library, T.
85 Impact/Simon Shepheard, BL;
Bridgeman Art Library/Oriental
Museum, Durham University, MR.
86 Format/Raissa Page, BL.
86-87 Network/Gideon Mendel, T.
88 Robert Harding/E. Simanor, BL.
88-89 Michael Freeman, T. 89 Sonia
Halliday, TR; Bridgeman Art Library,
BL. 90 Bridgeman Art Library/
British Library, TR; E.T. Archive, BL.
91 Keystone/Sygma, BL. 92 Format/
Brenda Prince, ML; Rex Features,
BR. 92-93 Magnum Photos/Fred
Mayer, T. 93 E.T. Archive, BM.
94 Bridgeman Art Library/Musee
Conde, Chantilly, TR. E.T. Archive,
BL. 95 Bridgeman Art Library/
Lambeth Palace Library, London.
96 Sonia Halliday, BL. 96-97 Roger
Hutchins, M. 97 Sygma/Jamel Balhi,
TR. 98 Trip/H.Rogers, TR; Magnum
Photos/Fred Mayer, BR. 99 Trip/ E.
James, TL; Hutchison Library/Liba
Taylor, B. 100 Format/Brenda Prince,
BL. 100-101 Sygma/J.P. Laffont, T;
Sygma/Daniel Mordzinski, B.
102 Hutchison Library/Liba Taylor,
BL. 102-103 Trip/H.Rogers, T.
103 Hutchison Library/Liba Taylor,
BR. 104 E.T. Archive/Bibliotheque
de l'Arsenal, Paris, TR; Trip/H. Rogers,
BM. 105 Sonia Halliday/Barry Searle,
BL; Sygma/Daniel Mordzinski, TR.
106 Format/Meryl Levin, BR.
106-107 Network/Barry Lewis, T.
107 Robert Harding/ASAP/Aliza
Auerbach, BR. 108 Bridgeman Art
Library/Giraudon/Louvre, Paris, B.
109 Hutchison Library, TL; Magnum
Photos/Stuart Franklin, BL. 110 Tim
Slade, TR; E.T.Archive/Bibliotheque
de l'Arsenal, Paris, B. 111 Michael
Holford, TR; Bridgeman Art Library/
Bibliotheque Nationale, Paris, BL.
112 *Christ in the House of his
Parents* by Millais/Tate Gallery, TR;
Baptism of Christ by Piero della
Francesca/Bridgeman Art Library/
National Gallery, London. 113 *The
Feeding of the Five Thousand* by
Hendrik de Clerck/ Bridgeman Art
Library/Kunsthistorisches Museum,
Vienna, TL. 114 Bridgeman Art
Library/Musee Conde, Chantilly, TR;
Sygma/E. Pasquier, BM. 115 *Christ
Mocked; the Crowning with Thorns* by
Hieronymus Bosch/E.T. Archive/
National Gallery, London, TL.
116 Trip/D. Butcher, BL; *The Descent
of the Holy Ghost* by Sandro
Botticelli/Bridgeman Art Library/
Birmingham Museum and Art
Gallery, TR. 117 *The Creation of
Adam* by Michelangelo/Robert
Harding/Roy Rainford, T; *Lambeth
Apocalypse*/Bridgeman Art Library/
Lambeth Palace Library, BL.

118 Robert Harding TR; Trip/A.
Tjagny-Rjadno, BL; 119 Collections/
Geoff Howard, TR; Sonia Halliday,
BL. 120 Robert Harding, BR.
120-121 Robert Harding/E. Simanor,
T; Hutchison Library/Lesley McIntyre,
B. 121 Hutchison Library/Melanie
Friend, TR. 122 John Walmsley, BL;
The Light of the World by William
Holman Hunt/Bridgeman Art
Library/Keble College, Oxford, TR.
123 *The Adoration of the Magi* by
Hieronymus Bosch/Bridgeman Art
Library/Prado, Madrid, TL. 124 *The
Resurrection* by Piero della Francesca/
Bridgeman Art Library/Pinacoteca,
Sansepolcro, ML; Bridgeman Art
Library, TR; Magnum/Fred Mayer,
BM. 124-125 Altamont Press Inc.
USA, T. 125 Roy Williams, BM.
126 *St Francis Preaching to the Birds*
by Giotto/Bridgeman Art Library/
San Francesco, Assisi, TR;
126-127 Robin Carter/Wildlife Art,
B. 127 Hutchison Library/Lesley
McIntyre, BR. 128 Sygma/Ira Wyman,
BM; Sygma, TR. 129 Trip/S. Grant,
TL; Topham Picturepoint, BL.
130 Peter Sanders, TR. 131 Sygma/
S. Elbaz, BL; Bridgeman Art Library/
British Museum, T. 132 Hutchison
Library/Mary Jelliffe, TR; Michael
Holford, BL. 133 Sonia Halliday/
Topkapi Palace Museum, Istanbul.
134 Sygma/A.Gyori, TR; Peter
Sanders, BL. 135 Bridgeman Art
Library/British Library, L.
136 Bridgeman Art Library, TR;
Peter Sanders, BL. 137 Bridgeman
Art Library/Musee Conde, Chantilly,
B. 138-139 Peter Sanders, M.
139 Magnum Photos/Abbas, TL;
Frank Spooner, BM. 140 Peter
Sanders, TR; Magnum Photos/Abbas,
BR. 141 Sonia Halliday, Istanbul
University Library, L. 142 Format/
Impact, TR; Trip/H. Rogers, BL.
143 Trip/H. Rogers, TL; Trip, BL.
144 Hutchison Library/Isabella Tree,
BL; 144-145 Roger Hutchins, M.
145 Peter Sanders, TR. 146 Sygma/
Alain Dejean, TR; Impact/Mark
Henley, BR. 147 Magnum Photos/
Abbas, T. 148 Peter Sanders, BL.
148-149 Robert Harding, T.
150 Magnum Photos/Steve McCurry,
BL. 150-151 Network/Gideon
Mendel, T. 151 Sally Greenhill, BR.
152 Network/Homer Sykes, BM.
152-153 Sygma/Les Stone, T.
153 Sygma, BR.

Front Cover: Hutchison/Liba Taylor,
TL; Collections, TM; Tony Stone,
TR; Michael Freeman, B.
Back cover: Bridgeman Art
Library/Victoria & Albert Museum.